THAT MAD GAME

James D. Forman

THAT MAD GAME

War and the Chances for Peace

Charles Scribner's Sons   New York

327
FOR

This book is for Victor Streit.
In my childhood he was the golden warrior battling his way
through the morass of Guadalcanal. Today I know him as gentle
educator and missionary, a mirror of the paradox and the hope in
which this book was written.

Copyright © 1980 James D. Forman
Library of Congress Cataloging in Publication Data

Forman, James D
  That mad game.

  Bibliography: p. 207
  SUMMARY: Presents an overview of war and peace throughout
history and examines the causes of war and the attempts to eradicate
them.
  1. War—literature. 2. Peace—literature. 3. History,
Modern—literature. [1. War. 2. Peace] I. Title.
JX1953.F56   303.6′6   80–11600

ISBN 0-684-16509-0

1 3 5 7 9 11 13 15 17 19 F/C 20 18 16 14 12 10 8 6 4 2

Printed in the United States of America

War, that mad game the world so loves to play . . .

Jonathan Swift

Ode to Sir William Temple

Contents

War or Peace ?

Albert Einstein, often regarded as the finest mind of the twentieth century, was once asked why, if he could solve the secrets of the universe, he could not devise a plan for the prevention of war. His answer was that world politics was more complicated than the rules of physics. Questions of peace and war involve not only politics but biology, psychology, sociology, economics, and a host of other disciplines. The subject is, in fact, so complex that to attempt to attack it in one thin volume is to induce laughter. Still, the fact and paradox remain: although war is humanity's most ancient and dangerous foe, and although an endless amount of material on the subject is disgorged annually, few attempts are made to look at the causes of war and at what, if anything, is being done to eradicate them.

There is no magic key to unlock the subject. For every answer found, a myriad of new questions appears—but this in no way diminishes the need for asking. Before wandering off naked into this labyrinth, we should at least define the subjects of the search: what is war, what is peace. The vital importance of that quest must be stressed.

War is an all too common word. There are price wars, gang wars, wars of words, and wars on poverty—none of which relates to war in the classic sense. War involves killing. So does murder, but murder is never condoned by the social unit within which it occurs, and usually it is severely punished. Killing on behalf of the tribe or nation, on the other hand, has always been applauded. War, then, may be defined as combat between trained members of large human groups using deadly weapons, with the support of their respective noncombatant populations, for the purpose of forcibly readjusting their relationships. Viewed in that context, there is scarcely a human society that has not devoted the major part of its collective energies to the preparation for and waging of war. This is as true today as it was six thousand years ago when humans first left the relative peace of the jungle to become "civilized."

Civilized man, though his history is one of war, has always dreamed of peace. When not gripped by war fever, most nations will solemnly agree upon the utter desirability and sanity of peace. *Peace* is as easy a word upon the tongue as *war*. The Belgian foreign minister Paul-Henri Spaak once remarked that he knew enough English to call for perpetual peace but scarcely enough to order a cucumber sandwich. Peace can be defined superficially as the absence of war. When nations are not fighting, they are at peace. But is peace no more than a respite between rounds? Will a "cold war" or "armed peace" such as we have today between the United States and the Soviet Union suffice, or does real peace imply genuine concord between national groups, with total and general disarmament? If so, it is something the civilized world has known only in Utopian theorizing. The Romans had a saying, *Si vis pacem, para bellum,* ("If you want peace, prepare for war"). It is a theory still accepted by the powers that be, though in practice it has done nothing but ensure the eventual occurrence of ever more cataclysmic wars. Humanity always seems ready to fight to the death for peace, seldom to live peacefully for it. There are many who would support William James's words: "Every up-to-date dictionary should say that 'peace' and 'war' mean the same thing. . . . It may even reasonably be said that the intensely sharp competitive preparation for war by the nations is the real war, permanent, unceasing, and that the battles are only a sort of public verification of the mastery gained during the 'peace' interval."

Even more pessimistic is the nineteenth-century French philosopher Pierre Joseph Proudhon: "Peace presupposes war: war presupposes peace. . . . And so, war and peace are correlative occurrences, equally valid and necessary, essentially the two principal functions of mankind. They alternate in history, as in the life of the individual . . . losing his strength and renewing it, as in political economy . . . production and consumption." Yet both James and Proudhon hated war.

The vast majority of mankind professes to loathe and condemn war. Still we fight as never before, at the rate of nearly three wars per year throughout our five thousand–plus years of recorded history. The pace is by no means constant; it is accelerating. According to one statistical survey, the sixteenth century endured a mere 87 battles. The eighteenth century experienced some 781, while the first forty years of the twentieth century, with World War II just starting, had already enjoyed 982 battles. Since that war the number of sovereign nations in the world, each capable of waging war, has doubled. The question arises whether the human race is destined to divide endlessly until we are once more chattering bands of hairless apes throwing coconuts at each other.

Over the long haul of history, however, wars have had entirely the opposite effect. Consequences have seldom been uniformly negative. War has been the occasion for social solidarity, cooperation, and the organizing of larger and larger human groups. Cooperation requires brains, and the more cooperative the group the greater its success in war. It was this talent for organization that made the Roman Empire a success.

All would agree that if a war is to be fought, it is better to win than lose. The loser is apt to suffer heavier casualties, surrender territory and booty, and perhaps become vassal to the victor. Some have argued that wars run counter to the rule that the fittest survive, for it is the fittest who die in battle. But there are always survivors, particularly on the winning side. Even within their own tribe, successful warriors tend to have priority where women are concerned, so war, at least in its more primitive form, can be said to have served the process of evolution well enough. Though not so strongly condoned in recent times, the doctrine "to the victor belongs the spoils" has resulted in territorial growth that has changed the course of world history. A study made by *Fortune* magazine as long ago as 1935 chided the smug American self-image as champion of peace and freedom in light of the fact that, during its relatively short history, the United States had seized from our native Americans, in one Indian war after another, 3,100,000 square miles of the earth's surface, second only to the British Empire's 3,500,000. Since that survey, the British Empire has ceased to exist, but if the old rules of the game of cooperation and conquest still applied, it would be reasonable to project the expansion of the United States until worldwide dominion ushered in the millennium of lasting peace.

However, in the summer of 1945, when the first atomic bomb was exploded, the time-honored rules ceased to apply. There have been sad jokes about a cave man, having invented the first bow and arrow, declaring that with such a terrible weapon in existence, war would no longer be possible. Similar words were recorded upon the invention of firearms, the airplane, and poison gas, but until the atomic bomb it remained possible to assess the cost of war cold-bloodedly against the possibly favorable results. The United States, with its relative isolation, has always had a militarily easy time of it, for the most part conducting its campaigns—win, lose, or draw— upon foreign soil.

That would not be the case with a thermonuclear war, the destructiveness of which is almost unimaginable. The mind boggles, simply refusing to accept the fact that one super-bomb contains six times the destructive power of all projectiles fired in all wars since the invention of gunpowder. In the nuclear stockpiles of the United States and the USSR there is set aside an atomic equivalent of twenty tons of TNT for the incineration of every human on the face of the globe. Every minute of every night and day, while we sit in school, commute to work, watch television, eat, and sleep, these weapons are aimed at their targets, at us and at them, aimed and firable at the touch of a button. This is a monumentally distressing thought, the sword of Damocles nightmarishly enlarged. Yet we live with it and, for the most part, forget about it.

Though war is not what it was, nor ever will be again, we go on talking about it in terms of the same old attitudes, using words like *pride* and *glory* and *courage*. We live surrounded by tributes to wars of the past. The artists of the world have devoted their energies to depicting the heroism and dedication of war. The Church has bestowed its blessing on war; the state, its rewards. The old modifiers survive, and we are lulled into thinking of war in the same old way, as something that can be won at modest sacrifice, while what it now really involves is the extinction of all living things, plant and animal. For such a worldwide atrocity the word *war* is obsolete, inadequate, and dangerously lulling. *Megadeath* and *race suicide* have been suggested as substitutes, but neither have the catchy quality of *war,* which should best be stricken from the dictionary.

If war has become totally suicidal and thus unacceptable as a method of social change, the alternative has to be total peace. Today the prospects for peace are synonymous with prospects for human survival. Formerly the morality of brotherly love, to be one's brother's keeper, was a mandate for self-improvement. Today it is a matter of self-preservation. It is no longer good enough to say, "I won't destroy the world unless someone else starts it." From something for which people yearned, peace has developed into a necessity. This does not mean peace in a completely tranquil and Utopian sense. It is unlikely that we shall ever be saints or that humanity will ever exist free of governmental controls, as anarchists and Communists suppose. Peace is never apt to be a static thing. It would be totally naïve to expect an entirely conflict-free society. Violence is not infallibly bad. Conflict—intellectual, political, artistic—is often highly productive. Strife and competition are too much a part of human nature, and human societies are too divergent and imperfect to expect, or even want, the perpetuation of the status quo, which often seems the objective of U.S. foreign policy. But if change is desirable and inevitable, it need not take the form of war or violent revolution. There are other ways of adjusting the world power structure. To contemplate a warless earth is to suppose a new kind of world order, supervised by some supreme social organization capable of administering a pervasive system of law and order that allows for change, conflict, and conflict resolution without resort to weapons. The modern world has already achieved huge adjustments, for the most part without violence. If sanity prevails, the future may still be bright, but the past is ominous. The problems of today's crowded globe are enormous. Its many sovereign states, all potential war-makers, are far from surrendering any of their sovereignty voluntarily. There will be no final answers here, but the past can be examined for its lessons and the present for its trends. Taken together, they may support some rather tremulous hypothesis concerning the future and whether mankind's final statement on the subject will be one of peace or war.

ONE

The Clatter of Arms

The clatter of arms
drowns the voice of the law. . . .

Montaigne, *Essays,* III, i

"War alone brings all human energies to their highest tension and sets a seal of nobility on the peoples who have the virtue to face it." So declared Benito Mussolini in *The Doctrine of Fascism,* a major stepping-stone on the path to World War II. It is, of course, pure speculation, but might he not have modified this assessment in 1945 after partisans had battered him to death and hung him by the heels from a gas station marquee? Unfortunately, the dead remain speechless. The voices raised in war's vindication are the unscathed, and they are many, regaling us with war's heroism, romance, and poetry. The subject is as inexhaustibly entertaining as sex. General William T. Sherman, having done his best to lay waste the South in the Civil War, expressed the contrary view succinctly: "War is hell." Clearly he recognized the problem but did nothing to explain or cure it.

Since its beginning at an uncertain date in human evolution, war has had numerous common threads that weave back and forth through the loom of history to the present day. The pattern may well continue in nonatomic so-called limited wars for centuries. Some features of the design remain constant, others come and go. The concern here is with these social, economic, and religious aspects of war rather than the continuing technical refinements in the arts of killing that have led to the novel impasse created by atomic power.

There are single-cause theories about war, such as: "Man is an aggressive animal and must fight," or "Economic inequality leads to class warfare," or "An army is nothing but a crowd, and war is two crowds mutually devoted to turning each other into a heap of corpses." All such limited theories may have relevance, but no single-cause theory is adequate. War is a phenomenon deeply inbred in the human experience. It is made up of innumerable fibers, and to fix on any one as the explanation would be a deception. Only by accepting the multiplicity and interrelations of causes can it be viewed realistically, let alone understood.

Origins of War

Wars have been described as red splashes on the title pages of human history, and they have certainly been with us for as long as mankind has kept records. How long before that is a matter of keen debate. Ants and rats have been accused of making war, but certainly never with humanity's premeditation. Some zoological observers have characterized the quarreling of various groups of apes as warfare, but if so, the casualties are at the barroom brawl level. Sigmund Freud should have known better when he stated, "Man is a wolf to man." Not at all. Wolves prey on other species for nourishment, as do all predators, including man, but like most animals, among their own kind wolves are pacifists. Mankind is the only species that collectively fights with malice aforethought, which is a cruel penalty for developing a large brain. Other creatures are simply not capable of collectively planning ahead. Although chimpanzees have been observed making elementary tools, they are incapable of creating long-range weapons.

Of course, man, inherently weak and lacking the natural armor of some species, would not have prevailed without his inventions. Only with a weapon lodged securely in his fist could he step forward as the most efficient and bloodthirsty predator on earth. Unfortunately, primitive weapons that were substitutes for claws and saber teeth have gone beyond the needs of a hungry predator, and herein zoologists have suggested a tragic flaw in man's nature. Animals inherently supplied with lethal weapons, such as the tiger and the wolf, seem to have built-in restraints that limit their intergroup fighting to contests that establish dominance between its members, without often causing serious injury or death. Other creatures, inherently less dangerous, such as rabbits and doves, may occasionally fight to the death because they lack such natural inhibitions. Man has been classed with this group. By nature he is not a killing machine, but, lacking instinctive restraints, he uses his unnatural weapons to the death. So the spear and the stone hand-ax may have ensured human survival when they were invented, but, given man's nature, his modern weapons are quite capable of reversing the process.

Just when man turned his innovations to self-destruction is a hotly debated subject. Modern man emerged physically about forty to fifty thousand years ago. Some observers assume he was already a warrior, but there is no solid evidence to support this. At that time he obtained nourishment by hunting and gathering. The social unit was probably a migrant tribe of no more than fifty humans, including children, the largest number that could live on the game in a hunting range. Such clans undoubtedly came into occasional collision, and may on those occasions have fought collectively, but organized killing as a community objective is uncommon among primitive peoples today and was undoubtedly rare then. They simply lacked the political organization or motivation. People with a nomadic foraging economy do not possess a home territory to protect or enlarge. There are no hoarded valuables to pillage. Even the acquisition of slaves served no practical purpose, as the economies were so unproductive that captives would eat up all that they might contribute to the foraging group.

Nevertheless, if the hunter-gatherer was at most a casual warrior, he was not idle in preparing himself for the bloody work that lay ahead. As a hunter, he was constantly refining his weapons, the first of which was a hand-held flint bludgeon or stabbing spear. Centuries later came the bow and arrow, and suddenly man was no longer restricted to the surrogate tooth and claw. Also armed with the less-efficient throwing spear, he could now deal death at a distance, and for the first time he stood apart from his rival predators. Having made him supreme as hunter, the bow also rendered him much more deadly as a warrior.

One puzzling event occurring approximately 35,000 years ago during the Pleistocene period has been used to suggest that our hunting-gathering forebears were indeed chronic warriors. At about this time Cro-Magnon Man arrived in Western Europe and Neanderthal Man vanished from the scene. Some have called this transition the original act of cannibalistic genocide. Undoubtedly there were clashes. Groups of significantly different appearance must occasionally have fought, but to imagine a wide-spread war of conquest and extermination seems farfetched. Even in the relatively short period of the American Indian Wars, the Indians suffered more from their susceptibility to unfamiliar diseases such as measles than they did from the white man's superior weaponry.

Civilization and War

For the most part, a world population of perhaps five million Stone Age humans kept busy hunting and gathering food. Somewhere along the line, dogs joined them as hunting companions. As long as there was sufficient game there was no pressure to change life-style, no need to pillage from other hand-to-mouth tribes. A change occurred when a drier climate following in the wake of the last Ice Age must have diminished the forests and cut back on the game. Then man was obliged to adapt or perish. The challenge was met by turning random gathering into active cultivation. Along with agriculture came the domestication of animal food. The first outlines of what would become modern civilization appeared about eleven thousand years ago. Roaming hunters were gradually becoming farmers and herders, with flocks of sheep raised as early as 9000 B.C. in northern Iraq, cattle and pigs perhaps two thousand years later.

What archaeologists call the Proto-Neolithic period had begun, and man's further evolution, which to this point had been largely a matter of biology, now became one of culture. Never before had humanity transformed nature for its own use. Science, technology, and modern war were born together on the high plateaus of Iran, spread steadily to the twin-rivers area of Mesopotamia, then gravitated southwest to the Nile and east to the Indus. Lifted above hand-to-mouth subsistence, human population for the first time increased rapidly. Villages, presumably limited in size by the problems of access to pastures and fields, probably housed about five hundred persons, a considerably larger community than the hunting pack. Until the eighteenth century and the Industrial Revolution, the bulk of the world's population continued to live in agricultural villages numbering a few hundred souls.

No longer did man live day to day. He could lay food aside. He could exchange surplus food for formerly unknown luxuries. He could, as never before, become unequal to his neighbor. He could envy, and it is appropriate that the initial violence recorded in the Bible is an allegory of the wars to come. Abel, the herder of sheep, is killed by his jealous brother, Cain, the farmer. Such "range wars" must have been increasingly common, and with food hoarded against the future, men could band together into primitive armies, brawling for the richer soil, the greener grazing land. If a certain group of people inhabit a Garden of Eden and are surrounded by hungry, shabby strangers, sooner or later they will have to fight or give way. A common need fought over by both farmers and herders was water access, and the English words *rivalry* and *river* have a common Latin root, *rivus*.

Once group fighting became frequent, clearly the larger and better-organized units prevailed. Discipline is the key to any successful army. The old easygoing democracy or communism of the wandering hunters had to yield gradually to a hierarchy of privilege, with central control and division of labor. Whatever man's nature, his propensities for making war seem in direct proportion to the degree his civilization is specialized. The more rigid the class structure, the more warlike the people. At the head of these societies would be the men of power, the kings, priests, and military elite. No better techniques availed for securing and enriching their status than conducting perpetual battles against nomadic tribes, neighboring villages, and, later, competing cities. Thus dynasties were formed, and by 3000 B.C. the city-states of the Middle East were organized militarily and industrially to a degree comparable to that of our modern era.

To survive was to be victorious, and the warriors who prevailed over their enemies gained esteem, booty, and bigger harems, presumably spreading the genes of their better-organized and warlike groups among the females of their routed foes. Whereas fighting among hunting bands, when it had occurred, differed little from shooting or bludgeoning game, village life changed fighting into an ongoing social institution, without which the group would lose vitality and its leaders might fall. Nor was war a static business of maintaining the status quo. Population was rapidly growing. Groups increasingly encroached upon each other's territory, and the city-state, if it did not want to decline, looked abroad for raw materials, slaves, and tribute.

Not until the Renaissance would there be a time of such rapid progress. The sailing ship was invented. Metal was mined and smelted. The wheeled vehicle and the plow came into use. Wars raged. Sumer, Ur, Babylon, and ancient Egypt rose, terrorized their neighbors, and fell. Gradually the focus of innovation and successful warfare shifted westward toward Europe, which had iron in its bogs and charcoal for smelting it in its forests, for without iron there could not be such a phenomenon as modern war.

Rituals

Civilization as we know it was by this time thoroughly launched, and man has been fighting ever since. The stakes in the game have immeasurably increased over the centuries, but certain rules have remained. First of all, there is justification. Long before Christianity invented the hypocrisy of the "just" war, men needed to explain their violence, if only to secure the support of their tribal gods. The God of the Hebrews went so far as to impel Israel's enemies into battle so they might be utterly annihilated (Joshua 3:10). Hitler's dark legions marched to battle with their belt buckles confidently emblazoned *"Gott mit uns"* ("God with us").

Beyond simply eliciting divine support, there is normally some rational vindication: self-defense, the moral depravity or worthlessness of the foe, the need for living space. The short-

term and very ancient provocation might be called *First Blood.*
Under the rules of First Blood, a member of one tribe or nation, not necessarily an important member, must be killed and
the death attributed to the prospective enemy. Never was
there a more succinct exchange on this subject than just before
World War I when British General Henry Hughes Wilson
asked, "What is the smallest British force that would be of any
practical assistance to you?" and France's General Ferdinand
Foch replied, "A single British soldier—and we will see to it
that he is killed." By Germans, of course. Sometimes First
Blood involves more than one person, and sometimes it is a
very valid reason, such as the attack on Pearl Harbor in World
War II. Often it is trumped up, as with the explosion of the
battleship *Maine,* which, nearly a century later, seems to have
been the result of an accidentally exploding boiler rather than
Spanish treachery. The important thing is that some member
of the group is dead, and that this death was caused by
"them," the enemy. Hitler, a superb propagandist, attempted
to gain public support for unleashing the Second World War by
cynically murdering several prisoners near the Polish border
and dressing their bodies in military uniforms, as though they
had been killed in a Polish attack. Secret German dispatches at
the time referred to this undertaking as "Operation Canned
Goods," which is as fitting as any other way to launch
history's most destructive war to date.

Among primitive peoples, war and weapons have always
been the exclusive business of the male. In particularly warlike
tribes, this rule is strictly observed. Societies in which the
tasks of men and women are less rigidly assigned are usually
more peaceable. Today, with the acceptance of total war,
women have gradually made inroads into military service. For
the most part combat remains a male prerogative, but the trend
is a novel and perhaps hopeful sign of a growing peaceable
spirit.

Once war is in the air, there are numerous symbols and rituals to be hauled out. The most primitive tribes have war dances to unify emotion and elicit divine support. Warriors brandish war clubs, old chiefs express their envy of the young and their regret at not joining in the fight. Man will fight individually when frightened or provoked, but, savage or civilized, it usually takes considerable drum-beating and parading about and speechmaking to put men collectively in a fighting mood.

From earliest times the military has been associated with myriad symbols. A tribe or clan had its own sign, such as an eagle or a thunderbolt, its power to be magically infused into the fighting men. Egyptian warriors carried ferocious animal totems. The Crusaders had their cross. Later came national flags, and even in sophisticated times great passions attach to these rectangles of colored cloth, as evidenced when Vietnam protestors burned "Old Glory." War songs serve the same unifying purpose, from the Yanomamo "I am a meat-hungry buzzard" to our own "Star-Spangled Banner." Germany's *"Deutschland über Alles"* has survived two costly wars that tended to prove the contrary. Music as a stimulant to the fighting spirit has always been an important part of war from primitive war drums to Egyptian tambourines and the Israelite trumpets that were credited with toppling the ancient walls of Jericho. The skirling of Scottish bagpipes has filled Highlanders with a sense of invincibility from the moors of Culloden to the desert of Al Alamein. Psychologically more personal is the military uniform, which, be it feathers and paint or shoulder patches and brass buttons, has caused the warrior to submerge his identity into that of the fighting group as a whole.

One particularly persistent characteristic of men in war is the need to assert their own strength while indicating the weakness of the enemy. This is done by tallying the enemy slain, whether by collecting wagonloads of Philistine foreskins in biblical times, scalps, or ears, or simply by making a body count, which can still be recalled as the gloomy leitmotiv of the Vietnam War.

Finally, there are the rituals enacted upon the conclusion of a successful campaign. Old in origin is the victory feast where the warlord assembles his fighting men in celebration. This helps to reassert a sense of unity when the group might otherwise tend to break apart. Psychologically it is a way of asserting the group's strength in contrast to the weakness of the defeated. For the heroes there are rewards: a crown in ancient Greece, a fine sword and order of knighthood for the Crusader, medals, pensions, and educational grants in current times. Until relatively recent times, outstanding warriors had the pick of the captive women, a practice no longer encouraged and usually occurring now only in spontaneous outbursts as in the Soviet Army's sack of Berlin at the close of World War II. Victorious generals had their triumphs and processionals and can still expect tickertape parades, honors, and, often, high office in the civilian world. Yet the tendency to glorify past wars with triumphal arches, cannons on the green, and bronze tablets listing "those who gave their lives" has diminished in recent years, a hopeful sign. The most vivid monuments to World War II are the preserved extermination camps in Europe and the skeletal remains of buildings in the heart of Hiroshima.

The Relevance of Today's Primitive Cultures

In considering the roots of war, one hotly contested approach is drawing inferences about the conduct of our ancient ancestors from studies of primitive peoples, the so-called living fossils who still inhabit remote corners of the globe. No blanket rule applies to today's few surviving primitives. They appear to run the gamut from natural pacifists to total warriors. Where organized fighting does take place, it is a far more personal business and an ongoing way of life motivated by the prospects of revenge, booty, and glory rather than the absolute conquest of the enemy or the seizure of his territory.

"If you sleep late, the enemy will come and kill you. If you are awake, you can face your enemy and die like a man," is the cheerful slogan of the Navajo people, who, before their subjugation by the white man, were compulsive warriors. However, compared with the Jivaro Indians of Ecuador and Peru, the Navajos were mild-mannered blanket-makers. Tribal war is the Jivaros' way of life. Boys at an early age accompany war parties to familiarize themselves with the bloody work that lies ahead. Coming of age involves a three-day feast, featuring a narcotic drink called *maikoa* which it is hoped will produce terrifying visions of "the old ones," the spirits of ancestors who will inspire the candidates to become powerful warriors. "I drink *maikoa* in order to kill my enemies" would be the Jivaros' summation.

The Jivaros' whole life-style is war-oriented. Entire tribal groups cluster together for protection in communal houses, usually situated on defensible hillsides. Surrounding banana plantations are further protected by high fences, and the approaches bristle with hidden traps.

Enmity between tribes is taken for granted, and even the natural death of a war chief or important warrior is attributed to the magical intervention of an enemy. Revenge follows so automatically that a Jivaro, if reprimanded for murder, is baffled. "He killed himself" is the way a Jivaro regards such retaliatory murders. Once a target for revenge has been selected, the prospective warriors exhort themselves with a spear-brandishing war dance which, if properly conducted, will guarantee victory. As many of the enemy tribe are slaughtered by stealth and treachery as possible, by hard fighting if need be. There is much fame and glory in bringing home severed heads, particularly when the souvenir belonged to a worthy foe. Then it is thought to ensure wealth, victory in future battles, and long life—expectations seldom fulfilled, especially since the Jivaros began substituting firearms for traditional spears. The increased killing capacity of the rifle has strained the old rules of the game to such an extent that the Jivaros have come very close to rendering themselves extinct.

Between the polar extremes of all-war and all-peace are the ritual warriors. Among such peoples war comes close to being a game, with aggression usually released harmlessly. Honors and trophies are taken with few fatalities, in conduct akin to what William James called the moral equivalent of war. Contests between certain tribes may involve only the use of thin sticks, with the whole business called off at the first sight of blood. Fighting to kill is a mystery to such people as the Baiga, a hunting-gathering people of central India. Wanting to aid their British friends during World War II, the Baiga took up a collection of bows and arrows to be presented to the British Army. When informed that the battles were being fought with guns, the Baiga were astonished: "If you use guns, people will really get killed." They could only rationalize such insanity as God's way of equalizing things. Whereas the Baiga had to contend with wild beasts, hunger, and disease, God had sent the British the madness of total war to keep them from growing old in comfort.

Ritual war has its more deadly adherents. The Blackfoot Indians of the nineteenth century conducted war at two levels, neither of which involved the seizure of territory or the systematic annihilation of the enemy. Most commonly the Blackfoot warriors formed small raiding parties to steal horses. Horses meant wealth and high status within the tribe. Raiding was also great sport, especially if horses could be obtained without fighting. In the long run of horse raiding there was fighting and killing, and killing, as with the Jivaros, necessitated revenge, which entailed the traditional trappings of war. Garbed and painted for battle, the war party would circle the camp while the women and old men stood in the center, drumming and singing. Then the warriors would dismount and perform a prancing "Riding Big Dance." Once this pep rally ended, they would go off looking for scalps, which, if they were successful, they would proudly display upon their return, along with the occasional hand, foot, or head, as proof of their triumph. Grown weary of endless fighting, the older chiefs would eventually attempt to establish peace with their traditional enemies. Such efforts were short-lived, as the need for horses and status that only war could provide was ritualistically central to the Blackfoot culture.

Finally there are the peace lovers: not so much peace lovers as those whose tribal habits have never been rewarded by taking the warpath. For the most part, as with India's Baiga, simple survival amid cruel nature has proved sufficient challenge. The settlement of disputes and achievement of esteem have come through devices other than force of arms. The most popular example is the Eskimo. They are a peaceful, friendly, cooperative, and generous people, but they have their serious disputes and their occasional murder. Since singing ability outranks skill with weapons and can bring great prestige, disputes that among other tribal groups might institute endless blood feuds are settled by song duels. In a song duel, the contestants musically attack each other before an audience with lyrical insults. The cause of the dispute tends to be overlooked, and the party whose skill and wit delight the audience is declared the winner, a custom which the more "civilized" world might do well to emulate.

If an analogy is to be drawn between our own primal roots and today's living fossils, the conclusion has to be that the latter fill the entire spectrum from pugilism to pacifism. This does not happen to be the case once society has become highly organized: that is, civilized. Then war seems to become a dynamic part of the rise and fall of political groups, accepted at worst as an unavoidable evil, at best as the very purpose of the state, with perpetual peace relegated to a world of make-believe Utopias.

War Among the Ancients

Five thousand years ago, with the sudden growth of city-states, there were no ready-made rules for international relations, no televisions or telephones, no trained diplomats. Illiteracy was universal. All men were enemies until proven otherwise, and the expanding city-states or displaced nomadic tribes were in constant ferment, contesting the diminishing milk and honey of the few promised lands. An objective Bible reading from the stories of Moses and Joshua provides a lively account of these uncompromising times. Forgotten death struggles between such centers as Umma and Lagash differ little in their telling from the campaigns of World War II, except that present victory monuments refrain from the smug depiction of abject prisoners being brained with stone bludgeons. Today we are concerned about a possible bad press and prefer to disguise such behavior as the napalm killing of women and children with tasteful words such as *pacification*. Killing in ancient times was a far more personal activity, and, as already stated, almost exclusively a masculine function.

One theory holds that during the early centuries of soil cultivation the supreme divinity was female, representing life and fertility, and that societies were correspondingly matriarchal and relatively peaceful. The turnabout is seen poetically in the Babylonian Hymn of Creation, which depicts the rebellion of male gods against the great universal Mother, Tiamat. From then on, men sat upon the thrones of earth and upon the high thrones of heaven. For the most part these mortal rulers considered themselves divine and their gods devoted, having the mutual objective of vanquishing the enemy and the alien gods who supported his cause.

Fighting was perpetual. Not even death put an end to it. When a Scythian leader died, he marched into the great unknown guarded by fifty of his best warriors, killed and stuffed to accompany him, all of them mounted on their best horses, prepared in like manner for the unending war after death. Such ideas lingered. The Egyptians modified the savagery and filled their pharaohs' tombs with armies of clay effigies. Centuries later the seafaring Vikings dispatched their defunct chieftains in flaming longships.

A soldier's lot usually entailed more attractive rewards than accompanying a king in death. Apart from joining the priesthood, it was the only way to get ahead. The warrior caste preserved and served its jealous gods and its divine rulers. To do so well meant success in battle, and success in battle meant regular fighting lest the army grow stale. To the victors belonged the spoils: booty, glory, slaves, and the satisfaction of regarding the rest of the population—artisans, peasants, farmers, slaves—as inferior.

Thanks to this new division of labor, slavery was at last a practical institution. The slave could take over the ugly tasks such as building pyramids, and, as the cheapest source of manual labor, was one more incentive for marching off to war. Economic exploitation of the vanquished has remained an aspect of war over the centuries. Though making slaves of captives has been abandoned, the victors after World War I did their best to suck off Germany's vital economic juices. The policy boomeranged, first into the great worldwide depression, and from depression into World War II. Today's world economy is very much a sum of all its parts. Aware of this and fearing a repeat performance, the victorious Allies agreed to reconstruct Germany and Japan after World War II. This recognition that modern war has no economic winners, not to mention the possibility of no survivors, is the most promising conclusion to emerge after more than six thousand years of organized combat. Among the ancients, war, while dangerous, remained a source of vast profit, power, and fame.

If the arts of peace were minimal, the tactics of war were basic. The Greek poet Homer described the hacking crunch of human walls:

> As when two lines of reapers, face to face,
> In some rich landlord's field of barley or wheat
> Move on, and fast the severed handfuls fall,
> So, springing on each other, they of Troy
> And they of Argos smote each other down.

This was war in a butcher shop, made more horrible by the realization that to lose was tantamount to being slain in the field. Among the Israelites, "Thou shalt not kill" was an in-group commandment, and victory over aliens meant the wholesale slaughter of the defeated males and sometimes the women and livestock as well.

Countless warrior societies arose, flourished, accumulated enemies—inevitably too many to resist—and finally fell, the violence of their descent usually a reflection of the barbarity of their ascendency. The dreaded Assyrians were typical. Their seventh-century B.C. empire was in its time the greatest in the Middle East, but lasted less than seventy-five years. Of far greater longevity were the Egyptians. Not unlike their neighbors, they were a rigid military caste society led into battle by a divine pharaoh. It was not their well-organized military machine that accounted for Egypt's long survival but their relative isolation, thanks to desert wilderness, from the close-packed seethe of other Middle Eastern city-states.

This contest for "living space" sometimes took more all-embracing form. In approximately 2400 B.C. there appears to have been a general breakdown of civilizations. Suddenly Achaeans, Indo-Aryans, Mitanni, Hittites, and others appeared, as if responding to a vast migratory explosion of population from outside the boundaries of the known civilized world. Better documented was the violent shifting of peoples around 1200 B.C. Then Indo-Europeans flowed into the Mediterranean area. Linked to this upheaval was the collapse of the Minoan and Mycenean civilizations. Dorians and Ionians were propelled into the Aegean area. The city of Troy was gutted. The warlike Hittites, inventors of the iron sword, vanished from history. As far south as Egypt, Ramses III fought desperate battles against invaders described as "People of the Sea" and finally drove them back, evidently as far as Palestine, where they became the settled Philistines.

With the subsidence of the mysterious "Sea People," the focus of world power shifted westward to Greece, which we honor for its contributions to democratic government and philosophy. However progressive in some respects, Greece's early enlightenment in no way embraced the subject of war. Aristotle's "We make war for the sake of peace" has cynically echoed down the ages. Thucydides at least was honestly perceptive when he put these words into the mouth of an Athenian calling for the surrender of the island of Melos: "Of the gods we believe and of men we know that by the necessary law of their nature they rule whenever they can. . . . Right, as the world goes, is only in questions between equals in power, while the strong do what they can and the weak suffer what they must." Like other ancient peoples, Greeks fought for booty, called on their gods for support, and sacrificed prisoners to propitiate these gods well into the fifth century B.C. Never, despite their political acumen, were these ancient Greek city-states able to extend a common rule of law among themselves, preferring war, it seems, to peace. They only briefly joined in a common cause when menaced from afar, particularly by the Persians at Marathon in 490 B.C and again at Thermopylae in 480 B.C. In these engagements, considering their inferior numbers, the Greeks were surprisingly successful. This was due to better discipline and a generally higher level of group spirit, cooperation, and tactical skills that put Greece one step ahead of the old human-wall approach that had characterized military formations until this time. As the gifted general Xenophon phrased it: "The art of war is, in the last result, the art of keeping one's freedom of action." Originally the Greeks had resorted to the shoving-crowd assault, but to create a more governable mass they developed a formation called a *phalanx,* which consisted of massed files of heavily armored, spear-laden foot soldiers in a large rectangular pattern.

The traditional Greek phalanx reached its highest development among the Spartans, a name so synonymous with stern militarism as to require elaboration. The warrior caste system prevailed in more ancient civilizations. Some Greek city-states, including Athens, relied on militia, with youths being called up in times of crisis. The unique Spartan system expected all male citizens to be warriors, and they were so trained from childhood. The Spartans had no use for art or music and even declined to send athletes to the Pan-Hellenic games. The society existed solely for war. Those whom they had conquered, the so-called helots, worked as serfs upon the land. Puberty rites for the future Spartan warrior involved savage whippings from which boys often died, and if they perished without whimpering they were posthumously entitled "champions."

Those who survived made fearless warriors indeed, but attrition, as with the South American Jivaro, was high. The population declined and the very rigidity of the Spartan system made for its final eclipse in 371 B.C. at the battle of Leuctra. The Thebans, all too painfully familiar with the accustomed Spartan deployment, for the first time concentrated their attack on the Spartan right flank. As each Spartan had been rigidly trained to rely on the shield of the man to his right for protection, this novelty created a sense of defenselessness. The Spartan phalanxes were demoralized from right to left, and much of the heretofore invincible army was in panicked flight without having struck a blow.

Theban ascendency was short-lived. Twenty-two years after

he left Thebes, where he had been held hostage, a witness of the new tactics returned to Greece at the head of an army. This was Philip of Macedon, a military genius who did much to renovate the old phalanx. Having variously extended the lances of the first five ranks so that they made one impenetrable wall of points, he perfected his cavalry to harry the flanks of the presumably pinned-down enemy. It worked for Philip against his old mentors, and it worked even more spectacularly upon the plains of Asia for his son, Alexander. There were conquerors before Alexander but none alive to us as personalities. Others would emulate him in the centuries to come, but none would deserve the title of "Conqueror" so surely, nor is the world apt to survive another like him. Alexander led his armies halfway across the world, driven on by an unquenchable thirst for adventure and booty beyond the dreams of avarice. Only illness could stop them finally. Certainly the Persians could not. At Arbela, lined up in the time-honored formations, the Persians left 100,000 dead upon the field at the cost of 450 Macedonians. Persia, Syria, finally even ageless Egypt fell before premature death claimed Alexander. Even as he lay dying, a greater power was incubating, which would bring a sense of internationalism and a kind of peace that the civilized world has not known before or since.

Rome

The ancient world's greatest and last success story was Rome. Beginning as a den of outcasts and robbers, the first Romans seldom squabbled among themselves but acted out in deed if not word the slogan "Ask not what Rome can do for you but what you can do for Rome." They had no Alexander at first, nor did they want so supreme a commander. They elected consuls to lead them, and these they served with the dedication of warrior ants. For six hundred years, despite bloody power struggles, slave insurrections, and civil wars, Rome prevailed

against all foreign foes in a battling world, first as a republic
and, after Caesar, as a dictatorship. Such longevity derived
from unparalled group cooperation, highly trained individuals
functioning efficiently within an effective hierarchy of authority.

> The Roman soldiers, bred in war's alarms,
> Bending with unjust loads and heavy arms,
> Cheerful their toilsome marches undergo,
> And pitch their sudden camp before the foe.

So wrote the poet Virgil. A more literal reporter would have
noted the contents of the soldier's seventy-five-pound pack:
cloak, armor, shield, cooking pot, rations, ax, spade, sword,
spear, helmet, and two hefty palisades which, after a day's
march, he would incorporate into the earthworks of each
night's fortified camp. Never were Roman armies surprised at
night. If the camp was attacked, each man knew his position,
for each camp was laid out along identical lines. Units were
identified by colored and numbered shields. Blasts on the
cornu and tuba, forerunners of the bugle, called them rapidly
into prescribed positions.

Without tireless training, such precision would have been
impossible. The Roman citizen-soldier began his military service at age seventeen, taking it for granted that it was his privilege to campaign until he reached age forty-five, and thereafter
serve on garrison duty until he was sixty, a career few survived. Only citizens were so honored. Not for many generations were mercenaries and allies increasingly incorporated
into the army. Though accepted as a privilege, Roman soldiering was no picnic. Sturdy fitness was demanded. According to
the Greek scholar Polybius, sham battles were constantly
fought with weapons twice the weight of those wielded in combat. Of this training Josephus, the Jewish historian, recorded:
"The Romans are sure of victory, knowing well that they have
to do with men who are not their equals. And they cannot, as

we must allow, deceive themselves; for their exercises are battles without bloodshed, and their battles bloody exercises."

The price in terms of discipline was enormous. A soldier who accidentally strayed beyond the range of the tuba call might be crucified as a traitor. One Roman commander, Titus Manlius Torquatus, having issued an order forbidding single combat with the enemy, discovered that his son had defeated a Gallic chief in hand-to-hand fighting. Without hesitation the father ordered his son's execution. Sentries who fell asleep were stoned to death; cowards were executed.

Only in victory could a soldier find reward. Catiline, rallying his army on the eve of battle in 62 B.C., outlined what had long been the prizes of victory and the penalties of defeat: "I conjure you, therefore, to maintain a brave and resolute spirit; and to remember, when you advance to battle, that on your own right hands depend riches, honor, and glory, with enjoyment of your liberty and of your country. If we conquer, all will be safe; we shall have provisions in abundance, and the colonies and corporate towns will open their gates to us. . . . But should fortune be unjust to your valor, take care not to lose your lives unavenged; take care not to be taken and butchered like cattle, rather than fighting like men, to leave to your enemies a bloody and mournful victory." The speech was a model for subsequent commanders and, as it turned out, was not unduly pessimistic, for within twenty-four hours Catiline and most of his army lay dead upon the field.

It required more than disciplined foot soldiers to ensure the success of Roman arms over the centuries. A million Persians had been broken by Alexander's phalanxes. Now half a million Roman soldiers policed the world, and they did so because they were highly organized into legions that garrisoned the frontiers of civilization. As barbarian raids in one area became more oppressive, the straight Roman roads, many of which still exist, made it easy to concentrate several legions rapidly. Not even the phalanx was a match for the legion in the field.

Whereas the phalanx moved as one inflexible unit and became unmanageable in rough terrain, the open formation favored by the Romans has been compared in versatility to the human hand, with options of feeling out the enemy's weak points like exploring fingers, then quickly compressing into a solid fist when a hard blow was necessary.

Just as no large human group had ever achieved such an efficient level of single-minded cooperation, never before or since has a single group come so close to achieving world peace through force of arms. By A.D. 212 Roman citizenship spread around the entire Mediterranean basin, included much of continental Europe, England, North Africa, and the Middle East to the borders of India. Not only the legions but a complex legal, administrative, and commercial structure held together a myriad of peoples and cultures in the Pax Romana, an ideal of world unity, law, and order that has continued to inspire hopes for one world ever since. But in success there is complacency, and in complacency there is decay. The Roman Empire was in serious decline before Emperor Valens confronted the Goths at Adrianople in A.D. 378. There the Empire officially died, as barbarian horsemen overran the legions and slaughtered the Emperor and two thirds of his army. The fall of Rome began a long decline in the spirit of universalism that has not since been regained.

"Holy" Wars

Christianity, at its inception, was adamantly pacifistic. This conviction proved embarrassing as the new religion moved from the role of persecuted protest group to that of complete authority in all that remained of the Roman Empire, at its new capital of Byzantium (Constantinople/Istanbul). Beset by barbarians on one side and fanatical Persian sun worshipers and, later, Moslems on the other, the Christian Emperors, often generals in their own right, did their best to temper total war with Christian restraint. One of their more outstanding leaders, Belisarius, wrote: "The first blessing is peace, as is agreed upon by all men who have even a small share of reason. . . . The best general, therefore, is that one who is able to bring about peace from war." But the Pax Romana was not to be recalled. Byzantine writings on the subject of war and peace did little to further the cause of brotherly love. On the one hand are the strictly military treatises such as the *Strategicon* composed by the Emperor-general Maurice about A.D. 578, in which he called for an end to paid mercenaries and a return to universal military service for citizens. A well-intended but more dangerous path had been pursued by Emperor Constantine, who wrote: "The wise man will wage just wars . . . [but he will] lament the necessity of just wars, if he remembers that he is a man, for if they were not just he would not wage them."

Ever since Constantine got this idea to appease his Christian conscience, Christian nations have been slaughtering each other with the mutual conviction that they fight with God's blessing. Various criteria have been established to assess whether circumstances justify the resort to arms. A just war may be fought if (1) a just solution has been diligently sought by all other possible means, (2) if it is in defense of the morally preferable side, (3) if it is conducted without vindictive anger, and (4) if it is fought without harming noncombatants and with fair treatment of prisoners.

Unfortunately man has always had a talent for rationalizing the justice of his own cause. Having done so, he can undertake the slaughter of his foe with the righteous spirit of a priest exorcising the devil. Hear Martin Luther on the subject: "It is a Christian act and an act of love confidently to kill, rob, and pillage the enemy, and to do everything that can injure him until one has conquered him according to the methods of war. Only, one must beware of sin, and not violate wives and virgins." So pervasive has become this Christian dogma that even professed non-Christians find themselves obliged to vindicate their warmongering. Lenin, the patron of Russian communism, regarded any war that advanced the cause of world revolution as just. Modern wars are laboriously analyzed to claim the sanction of God or some higher morality, and cynical expressions to the contrary are regarded as in bad taste such as this humorous prayer attributed to John Benjamin: "Gracious Lord, Oh bomb the Germans, spare their women for thy sake, and if that is not too easy we will pardon thy mistake, gracious Lord, whate'er shall be don't let anyone bomb me."

An interesting footnote to the just-war idea flourished among Christian nations during the Middle Ages. That was the so-called Truce of God. Though wars among princes, barons, and assorted feudal lords were incessant, they were relatively moderate. The objective usually was aggrandisement, and the well-armored and wealthy participants generally suffered only bruises, capture, and ransom. The unpleasantness of slaughter was left to the peasant retainers who went into the fray without armor, horses, or the means to raise a ransom. Even so, the clergy did what it could with theological weapons to moderate and limit the fighting. Their achievement was the eleventh-century Truce of God, which restricted battle to certain weekdays and outlawed it entirely during sacred periods such as Lent. For the most part, the need for divine approval was not a moderating force, for once that sanction was officially obtained, all restraint was put aside and war was replaced by the crusade.

The first official Crusade was urged by Pope Urban II in 1095. He was a potent propagandist, as his words indicate: "The cause of these labors will be charity, if, thus warned by the command of God, you lay down your lives for the brethren; the wages of charity will be the grace of God; with confidence to attack the enemies of God! . . . The Turk never ventures upon close fight; but, when driven from his station, he bends his bow a distance, and trusts the winds to cause the wound he intends. As he has poisoned arrows, venom, and not valor, inflicts death on the man he strikes. Whatever he effects, then, I attribute to fortune, not to courage, because he wars by flight and by poison. It is apparent, too, that every race born in that region, being scorched with the intense heat of the sun, abounds more in reflection than in blood; and, therefore, they avoid coming to close quarters, because they are aware how little blood they possess. Whereas the people who are born amid the polar frosts, and distant from the sun's heat, are less cautious indeed, but, animated by their copious and rich flow of blood, they fight with the greater alacrity. . . . Let such as are going to the fight for Christianity put the form of the cross upon their garments, that they may outwardly demonstrate the love arising from their inward faith. Let them enjoy, by the gift of God and the privilege of St. Peter, absolution from all their crimes. . . ."

Before the Pope had finished, the crowd went wild, shouting, *"Deus volt"*—"God wills it." The crusading passion swept all the Christian world with a unity of purpose unknown since Roman times. Other churchmen rallied behind Urban II, and together they concocted masterly propaganda that even Hitler could not improve upon. Paintings, akin to modern posters, were circulated from town to town, depicting grotesque Saracens trampling on the Cross. Papal bulls, letters, poems went around. The English chronicler Matthew Paris recorded convincingly that the Moslems were poisoning pepper imported from the Orient. All this was necessary to generate a righteous mood, for in reality the Saracen custodians of the Christian holy places maintained them with respect and for a moderate tax protected visiting Christian pilgrims from local bandits to a degree unknown in Europe. Nevertheless, to the Crusader arriving before the walls of Jerusalem in 1099, the enemy was satanic. When the city fell, the victors waded through rivers of gore to the Church of the Holy Sepulcher. Raymond de Saint-Gilles observed, "It was a just and splendid judgment of God, that this place should be filled with the blood of the unbelievers, when it had suffered so long from their blasphemies."

The Crusades sputtered on for the better part of two hundred years. Incentives were enormous. St. Thomas Aquinas promised a "better world" for those who took part. St. Bernard did the same: "The soldiers of Christ can fight the Lord's battles in all safety. For whether they kill the enemy or die themselves, they need fear nothing. To die for Christ and to kill his enemies, there is no crime in that, only glory." If paradise were not enough, the participants were quick to realize that the Crusades offered untold booty, an appeal culminating in the perversion known at the Fourth Crusade. Though assembled in good faith, the expedition was quickly induced to ignore the Holy Land and turned its avarice instead upon Christian Constantinople. After months of siege, on a winter day in 1204 the city succumbed. Amid the pillage that followed, a great cultural heritage, including much that had survived from ancient Greece, was totally destroyed. The "just" war conceived in Constantinople had brought about its entirely undeserved ruin.

Despite such distortions, the concept of the just war outlived the official Crusades. It has infused succeeding wars to a greater or lesser extent with a sense of righteous wrath which, in practice, makes for bad judgment and brutality. Most nations have had their holy wars. In Islam the word is *jihad,* and a devout Moslem, like a Crusader, accepts the idea that paradise can be obtained by the selfless application of the sword. Such fanatical fervor survives in the words of the Ayatollah Khomeini spoken during his country's 1979 confrontation with the United States. "This is not a struggle between the U.S. and Iran. It is a struggle between Islam and blasphemy." Until after World War II the same spirit imbued the Japanese soldier dying for the divine Emperor. The great wars of the twentieth century, though complex in their causes, have not been lacking in crusading spirit. The evangelist Billy Sunday sounded like a poor man's Pope Urban II when he preached during the First World War: "The man who breaks all the rules but at last dies fighting in the trenches is better than you God-forsaken mutts who won't enlist." The First World War was officially christened "the war to make the world safe for democracy" by President Wilson, while in World War II General Eisenhower designated the final campaigns against Germany a "Crusade in Europe."

Yet in all this righteous fury there is hope. If we still labor over just wars, much passion has gone out of the purely holy wars. Had hydrogen bombs been available to the armored Crusader and his Moslem foe, human history might have terminated centuries ago. Today, essentially religious conflicts such as endlessly bring death to Catholics and Protestants in Northern Ireland are no longer a primary threat to world peace, and Arab-Israeli tensions are not so much religious in origin as territorial. For the most part, contradictory religious groups accept one another. In this spirit, Pope John XXIII, in the name of the Catholic Church, did much to eradicate the harm done by the just-war theory when he disavowed the distinction between just and unjust wars and branded all war in an atomic age as evil. The issue has since been debated, but the Vatican has continued to strengthen its new position, so that subsequent claims of fighting in God's cause must be made without official sanction.

War as the Sport of Kings

While the Crusades remain the classic example of religious war, man's relationship to his God excused many a European slaughter well into the seventeenth century. Gustavus

Adolphus of Sweden supported Protestantism against the Holy
Roman Empire with the words "Here strive God and the
Devil. If you hold with God, come over to me. If you prefer the
Devil, you will have to fight me first." With like conviction,
the English Puritan Oliver Cromwell put Ireland to the torch.
Then, with religious passion spent, came a near respite. The
monarchical state was by this time emerging from the Middle
Ages. Feudal armies were being replaced by standing armies
supported by taxes. Loyalty was to the king first and the country second, and it was now a difficult matter for a conspiracy of
lords to turn out their sovereign. As the Earl of Manchester
observed, "If we beat the King ninety and nine times, yet he is
king still, and so will his posterity be after him; but if the king
beats us then we shall all be hanged, and our posterity made
slaves."

In this newfound security upon the throne, European sovereigns could count on well-trained armies to carry out their military whims. War, despite the high wager in booty and empire,
was little more than a life-sized game of chess in which the
soldiers acted without asking to know why and without the
king's feeling he owed an explanation to his subjects. Whereas
battles had formerly concentrated on annihilation, by common
consent moderation became the goal. Victory was sought
through maneuver and siege rather than bloodshed, and the
civilian population was safe enough as long as it kept out of the
way. In the words of the Marquis de Vauban, "Our attacks
reach their end by the shortest, most reasonable, and the least
bloody methods that can be used."

If this seems a practical and businesslike way of conducting
war at the highest level, for many a common soldier war had
for some time been purely a way of earning a living. The soldier of fortune or mercenary is nearly as old as war, but as the
ambitions of Europe's royalty outstripped reserves of native
soldiery, the foreign mercenary came into his own. In the early
years they were little more than brigands hiring themselves out

for loot. The acute political philosopher Machiavelli entirely disapproved. "Troops of this sort are disunited, ambitious, undisciplined, and faithless, swaggering when among friends and cowardly in the face of the enemy. . . . If you lose with them you are undone, if you win you become their prisoner." Pillage and rape were deemed a proper reward for victory, and if mercenaries refused to fight there was nothing to be done, as when two parties of Swiss mercenaries hired by foreign kings declined to engage when called upon to oppose one another.

Long before the practical wars of the eighteenth century, mercenaries were incorporated into standing professional armies. Where they had formerly looked for the spoils of battle, they now fought for regular pay. By the time of the American Revolution the practice was so businesslike as to be almost ludicrous. Not wanting to waste his good British troops on rebels, King George III cast about for hirelings. Russia declined to provide the desired "gun fodder," but various deals were made with German princelings. The first to sign a contract, on January 9, 1776, was the Duke of Brunswick. Each soldier was to be paid at the customary rate expected by British troops. In addition, there was a fee for the Duke, which expressly provided that he should receive what amounted to $35 for every soldier killed and $11.66 for each man wounded. These troops, 29,867 of whom participated in the Revolution, have been remembered as Hessians because the largest single contingent was furnished by the Landgrave of Hesse-Cassel. No longer the brawling soldiers of fortune of former times but reluctant farm boys, they embarked so gloomily from Cassel that the expression "*Ab nach Cassel*" ("Go to Cassel") became a euphemism for "You've been sold out." With the Hessians plodding into history, the great days of the mercenaries were coming to an end. Yet the world has its mercenaries still, hardened professionals lured by exorbitant pay and the love of combat into the squabbles of newly emergent nations.

Empire Building

Five hundred years ago centers of civilization were few and isolated from each other. Then came the Industrial Revolution and the violent spread of Western European culture around the globe. Though the term *world war* was not yet coined, all the major nations of Europe were at war during the eighteenth century, and these engagements embraced Asia, Africa, and North and South America. Greed has ever been an inducement for men to fight, but never before had a system of industrial capitalism so intensified economic competition among expanding states on a world scale. Increased needs for markets, raw materials, and investment opportunities had turned the sport of kings into the broader commerce of empire building. Nothing so typifies this amalgam of crown policy, business opportunism, and war as the several East India Companies established by England, Holland, France, Denmark, Scotland, Spain, Austria, and Sweden. By far the most important was the English version, incorporated by Elizabeth I's charter on December 31, 1600. Trade wars with its European rivals encouraged the growing monopoly of the British East India Company, until the victory of Plassey in 1757 made the company, with its investors and private army, the ruling power in India. For a hundred years the company prospered by milking India of her resources. A mutiny on the part of dissatisfied Indians led to the involvement of the British Army and an official governmental takeover in 1858, with Queen Victoria becoming Empress of India in 1876.

In such manner the European state system annexed much of the undeveloped world. The process inevitably involved the two sorts of warfare experienced by the East India Companies and the states that supported them: first, wars of conquest against weak countries that could be exploited for their raw materials; second, trade wars between powerful European countries for control of the weaker countries.

Economic advantage remains a strong motive for going to war. With increasing shortages of vital raw materials such as petroleum, perhaps in the not too distant future even food, the pressures will certainly not diminish. Techniques have at least gained some subtlety. The seizure of real estate and direct dominion over its inhabitants has given way to the more nebulous establishment of "spheres of influence." During World War II the United States asserted its intention of making no territorial annexations. It did much to press the dismemberment of the Dutch, French, and British empires, while at the same time obtaining large markets and other benefits that had formerly flowed to Amsterdam, Paris, and London. The recent war in Vietnam, formerly French Indo-China, though characterized as a war to preserve the independence of a small friendly nation from Communist envelopment, was to a large extent prompted by a desire to maintain an economic sphere of influence in Southeast Asia. Similarly, behind much of the rhetorical facade, the continuing tension in the Persian Gulf has as its heart access to the rich oil supplies of the area.

The People Go to War

Up until the later part of the eighteenth century, war generally involved the king, his army, and private business interests. Power and money were at stake, and the fighting was done by professionals, often without disrupting civilians. But a change was brewing, one that would push the conduct of wars in the direction of increased savagery. An early voice recognizing war no longer as a royal prerogative belonged to Patrick Henry, speaking on March 23, 1775, just days before the outbreak of the American Revolution. "Three millions of people, armed in the holy cause of liberty, and in such a country as that which we possess, are invincible by any force which our enemy can send against us." The American Revolution was only one aspect of the larger world rivalry between France and

England which had festered for the better part of the eighteenth century, and which would continue until the final defeat
of Napoleon in 1815. To the American colonists who took part,
however, it was a very personal war, a people's war.

Although the American Revolution did much to initiate the
ideological warfare that has raged so savagely ever since, it
also demonstrated how thirteen potentially jealous political
units could combine into one Union, with a built-in mechanism
for mediating, short of war, disputes between sovereign states.
That device is the Supreme Court, and the system has worked
very well with the single exception of the Civil War. It gives
reason to hope that some more complex plan for world law and
order may one day be implemented.

The American Revolution was a moderate war in terms of
slaughter. The combatants were for the most part professional
soldiers, and a certain sympathy between Britain and her children never was exhausted. The real break with the past came
in France, where the rallying cry had been "Long live the
King." That affection was eroding in the eighteenth century
and there was the example of the American colonists who had
snubbed their sovereign and gotten away with it. New philosophies stirred the French people, none more powerfully than
Jean Jacques Rousseau's *Social Contract,* first published in
1762. The central idea was that men did not agree to obey a
ruler but agreed to subordinate their powers and rights to the
community as a whole. This was the democratic ideal, but in
France, which saw its society divided into three so-called es-
tates (First Estate, the clergy; Second Estate, a small clique of
nobility under the King; Third, the mass of the people), it was
the Second Estate that ruled and the Third that slaved and
starved. The year 1789 witnessed the explosion of the French
Revolution, the first thoroughgoing people's war. From the en-
suing bloodbath came ideas which, combined with events,
made for the terrible wars of the twentieth century.

All-important is the concept of nationalism, loyalty to a state of which one is a part, rather than to a sovereign to whom one is subordinate. This idea has been called today's idolatrous religion. Nationalism, and its wedding to the economic "ism," capitalism, has given birth to a number of fighting "isms," among which are communism and fascism, ideas for which untold millions have died.

With royalty discredited, war as the sport of kings fell into disrepute. From then on, it was the serious occupation of all the people. As such, the idea, if not the reality, of "total" war was voiced by the Prussian General Karl von Clausewitz (1780–1831), who said: "To introduce into the philosophy of war a principle of moderation would be an absurdity. War is an act of violence pushed to its utmost bounds . . . the military power must be destroyed, the country conquered so that it cannot produce a new military power, and even the will of the enemy destroyed." As Europe fell into the grip of the Napoleonic Wars, men were beginning to think of themselves as citizens rather than as subjects.

Napoleon

It seems an unfortunate fact of history that a people accustomed to dictatorial government can rarely manage democratically for long. This has been termed the *authoritarian culture lag*. Once the French Third Estate had the management of the state in its hands, it quickly transferred the responsibility, not back to the King, but to a soldier, Napoleon Bonaparte. Though he would become Emperor and more powerful than the kings before him, Napoleon shrewdly maintained the illusion of popular nationalism, as when he spoke to his troops on April 26, 1796: "Soldiers! Your country is entitled to expect great things of you. Will you justify her expectations? Your greatest obstacles are already overcome, but you have yet many battles to fight, many towns to capture, many rivers to pass over. Is there one among you whose courage fails him? Is there one, I say, who would rather retreat to the summits of the Apennines and Alps, and patiently endure the insults of the slavish rabble? No, no one among the victors of Montenotte, Millesimo, Dego, and Mondovi! All burn with the ambition to spread the fame of the French nation throughout the world; the desire of every one of you is to humble those proud rulers who would fetter us in chains."

In giving lip service to the concept of universal civic responsibility, Napoleon was able to achieve the fact of universal military conscription. Having ridden to power on the crest of a people's war, Napoleon could harness hitherto undreamed-of reserves of military, and hence political, power to his dreams of conquest. Against him were ranged at first states that believed that war was not the affair of ordinary citizens. Napoleon might have been the Moses to lead the troubled hordes of Europe to a new Promised Land, but he saw himself as a warrior, a successful one. Thus the French began to serve him rather than the political ideas from which he had sprung. As the wars went endlessly on, the tide in France reversed itself. The patriotic citizen army was gradually transformed into a professional one, as Napoleon began to overstep himself. His unjustified invasions of Spain in 1808 and Russia in 1812 inspired patriotic upsurges of nationalism in those countries which set Napoleon on the final path to Waterloo. His empire came apart in 1814, but loyalty to the nation/state/fatherland/*la patrie*/America the Beautiful—whatever a citizen cared to call that union of people which believes it constitutes a single nation—survived. With its survival came the conviction that this national unit should be free from control by alien states, a belief fortified for the most part by common race, customs, religion, language, and social and political traditions.

The American Civil War

The new idea of nationalism was no guarantee of solidarity within any given state. Social unrest continued to disturb the states of Europe but, in general, exhaustion from the Napoleonic Wars had restored a certain restraint in international affairs. Despite the retention of universal conscription, the armed hordes of 1812 were only a painful memory. Meanwhile, loyalties in the United States were dividing; the rural South began to see itself victimized by the industrial North. A Confederacy of Southern states formed in 1861 and was as quickly resisted by President Lincoln, whose words seem a reflection of the French Revolution: "I consider the central idea pervading this struggle is the necessity that is upon us of proving that popular government is not an absurdity. . . . If we fail it will go far to prove the inability of the people to govern themselves." Both sides fought with the absolute conviction of righteousness. In July 1861 two scarcely trained mobs of citizen soldiers battered each other at Bull Run. While the War of 1812 saw the sacking of the nation's capital, only 2 percent of American adult males took up arms. In the Civil War 10 percent fought, and for every 100 of these men, 13 were killed or wounded.

If the American Civil War did little to modify the idea behind national wars, in terms of weaponry and tactics it is the first conflict in history to be regarded as modern. The Napoleonic Wars had been successfully conducted with massed formations of men and guns, but, even as those battles rumbled, a Scottish clergyman was inventing the percussion cap, a means of igniting gunpowder instantaneously. It was the most significant advance in firepower since the invention of gunpowder. From this followed metallic cartridges, successful repeating rifles, and the rapid-fire Gatling gun. These, together with iron-clad ships, trenches, and wire entanglements, all had their baptism of fire in the Civil War. Combat was becoming uglier and more lethal than ever, yet veterans such as the much respected Justice Oliver Wendell Holmes, Jr., could look back and write: "War when you are at it is horrible and dull; it is only when time has passed that you see that its message was divine." Perhaps he is referring to the emancipation of the slaves, but even so there are, one hopes, few intelligent people left in the world who still see a divine aspect to modern war.

World War I: The Path to Total War

If the Napoleonic conflict had put a damper on militarism in Europe, the fires of nationalism were far from extinguished. Nowhere did they burn hotter than in the heart of German's Iron Chancellor, Otto Eduard Leopold von Bismarck, who in 1888 successfully called for a larger army budget: "If we in Germany should wish to wage war with the full exertion of our national strength, it must be a war with which all who engage in it, all who suffer themselves as sacrifices in it—in short, the whole nation—take part as one man; it must be a people's war." Bismarck did not live to see the day. He died in 1898, sixteen years before the beginning of the war for which he had prepared. Up until the last many believed it would not come, agreeing with Norman Angell's persuasive book *The Great Illusion* (1910) which asserted that there would be no more major wars because they were no longer economically profitable. But there were more prophetic authors writing at the same time, among them General Friedrich von Bernhardi, whose *Germany and the Next War* characterized war as a natural struggle for existence, an opinion which all too soon would be shared by Adolf Hitler.

When World War I came, it was, ironically, in the first instance an old-fashioned kingly war of empire. The balance of power in Europe had held for the better part of a century, but as with an earthquake belt, terrible pressure had been created by ambitious political, military, and industrial leaders on both sides. No pressure was greater than that exerted by Germany, which felt it had been denied its place as a colonial power in the world. "First blood" was shed by Archduke Ferdinand of Austria, and with this provocation came the deluge. Before the fighting ended in 1918, 1.4 billion of the world's total population of 1.6 billion people had come under a state of war. No nation that mattered or wanted to matter could now afford to ignore Europe's quarrels.

If the provocations were old-fashioned, private citizens on both sides were far from reluctant. During the mid-nineteenth century, popular unrest had come close to popular sovereignty in many of the countries of Europe, but for the most part the upheavals had fallen short and full power had returned to their rulers to engage in secret strategy and diplomacy. When the blank check was presented in the summer of 1914, it was enthusiastically paid, with interest. By that time, apart from the few who had engaged in distant colonial wars, only old men remembered actual combat. The thirst for war is always more urgent among those who have never savored it, and a young English poet, Rupert Brooke, could characterize this zeal for war as "swimmers into cleanness leaping." Where enthusiasm was not spontaneous, propaganda—speeches, posters, tracts, parades—drummed it up more energetically than at any time since the First Crusade. Men marched singing to the railroad stations with flowers festooning their rifle barrels. It was as though the right to fight, once the luxury of kings, was now a high privilege bestowed upon peasants and working men of all nations who instantly, passionately, and proudly identified with their own armies and navies. Even as Czarist Russia mobilized its forces and Germany rushed troops into neutral Belgium pursuant to a plan created by General Alfred von Schlieffen, both sides claimed a role of self-defense. Even before the first shots were fired, the guilt over which side started it was being hotly debated. The issue was only resolved by the winners and the blame, as always, fixed upon the vanquished.

In the United States there was general scorn for European quarrels. President Wilson was reelected in 1916 with the slogan "He kept us out of war." The popular song was "I Didn't Raise My Boy to Be a Soldier," and few were the voices of

derision who agreed with hell-for-leather Theodore Roosevelt
when he asserted that they might as well sing "I Didn't Raise
My Girl to Be a Mother." Attitudes began to change when the
tide of battle turned against the Allies. American banking
houses, which had made substantial loans to France and Britain, were the first to show concern. Whereas trade with the
Central Powers had declined from 169 million dollars a year in
1914 to but one million in 1916, thanks in part to the British
blockade, trade with the Allies had soared from 824 million to 3
billion during the same period, facts which left the American
business community with little doubt as to which side it favored.

Early in 1917 magazines and newspapers subjected the
American people to an unprecedented campaign of psychological bombardment, characterizing Germans as a barbarian
threat to the United States. Old stories, many of them false,
were reprinted describing German atrocities. Germany's declared intent to conduct unrestricted submarine warfare was
taken as a direct provocation. Much was made of the sinking of
the British ship *Lusitania*, which was carrying many American
passengers. The fact that it carried armaments as cargo, as
Germany claimed, was denied for many years. Martial music
blared across the land. On April 2, 1917, within six months of
being elected on a peace platform, President Wilson called on
the United States to fight a war that would "make the world
safe for democracy." The House of Representatives supported
him 373 to 50, a preponderance fairly representing the national
mood. Public passions, once the war was accepted, reached
absurd proportions. Sauerkraut, because of its German name,
was rechristened Liberty cabbage. Civilians were indicted or
imprisoned for the following: receiving a Red Cross solicitor in
a "hostile" manner; printing "We must make the world safe
for democracy even if we have to bean the Goddess of Liberty
to do it"; laughing at the inept drilling of recruits; spitting on
the sidewalk in the presence of Italian officers, our allies. Min-

isters were defrocked for recalling the Sermon on the Mount to their congregations, and college professors were fired after expressing pacifist sentiments.

Thousands of miles from the trenches, Americans could afford to vent their spleen in such superficial fashion, but for many a civilian in Europe the conflict offered a first terrible taste of total war. German General Ludendorff popularized the phrase with his treatise *Der Totale Krieg (The Total War),* in which he wrote: "Every individual in the nation is expected to give his entire strength either at the front or at home, and this he can only do when he realizes that it is an immutable and inviolate truth that war is being waged solely for the existence of the nation. A totalitarian policy must put at the disposal of such a war the strength of the nation and preserve it and only a conformity to the fundamental racial and spiritual laws will succeed in welding nation, conduct of war, and politics into that powerful unity which is the basis of national preservation." This was total war as conceived by Bismarck, complete civilian participation in forging the weapons of modern war, but not yet the next logical step, which would turn contributors behind the lines into legitimate targets.

In common with other combatants, Britain was obliged to employ thousands of women in war-related industries as the appetites of mechanized battle proved insatiable. From war work women gravitated to the first national corps of uniformed female volunteers trained as auxiliaries. They proved so useful that it can be fairly said that since 1916 woman's role in war ceased being a passive one.

A lesson of the American Civil War, that close-packed masses of flesh cannot stand against a hail of lead and steel, was not at first remembered. Repeatedly, the gallant charges of the past were launched. Rapid-fire weapons cut soldiers down until gradually they dug themselves into the earth, to live like moles in parallel lines from the Alps to the sea. Unabashed, the armchair generals who no longer shared the fate of their men developed the grotesque policy called *attrition*. This was the Allied euphemism for the more grisly German phrase *Blutpumpe* (literally, "blood pump"), which meant hurling living bodies into the maelstrom of mechanized destruction until one side, presumably the enemy, ran out of soldiers. Periodically one side, then the other, poured men and guns into this inferno. At Passchendaele 4.3 million artillery shells were fired in 100 days; 300,000 men died. The attack failed. At Verdun the French General Joffre exhorted his counterattacking troops: "Your élan will prove irresistible. It will take you at the first effort beyond the foe's fortified lines and to his batteries. You will then allow him neither truce nor repose until the victory has been achieved." A million Frenchmen died obedient to this exhortation, and still the lines held firm.

If the lingering romance of war perished during World War I, it died for one Englishman on July 1, 1916, the first day of the Battle of the Somme. The British assault began with a certain bravado. Captain W. P. Nevill of the 8th East Surrey Regiment had brought four soccer balls back from leave, one for each of his platoons. One ball bore the inscription, "The Great European Cup—The Final—East Surreys v. Bavarians—Kick off at 0." As the guns fell silent and a terrible stillness gripped the field, Captain Nevill, who had offered a prize for the group that first drove their ball to the German lines, climbed from the trench and kicked the first ball toward those distant German machine guns. Sixty-six thousand young Britons followed those bouncing balls. Before an hour had passed, half of them lay dead or wounded on the field—as many men as had followed Alexander the Great to conquer the world. The battle dragged on for weeks, accounting for over a million casualties before exhaustion brought an end to the fighting. Captain Nevill's prize went uncollected, as he had been among the first to fall. One regimental history summed up the day: "So Ends the Golden Age." Whether or not the age had been golden remains debatable, but certainly a good many golden illusions were fading.

By 1917 demoralization and even mutiny were rife. Apart from the inhuman conditions and the seeming futility of it all, there was the remoteness of those who gave commands. Since ancient times a respected commander was one who shared hardships with his men. Now, thanks largely to the vastness of the armies involved, directives came from far behind the lines. One high-ranking British officer, inspecting the situation after a disastrous battle, burst into tears and exclaimed, "Good God, did we really send men to fight in that?" Few were so compassionate. On the Eastern Front the huge Russian Army melted away. A wave of pacifism swept through the French Army and whole regiments refused to go forward. Only the enthusiastic arrival of the unbloodied Americans was able to tip the balance of disillusionment and bring an end to the war to end all wars.

Between World Wars

Victory turned out to be only the prelude to World War II, with the years between serving to clarify the full significance of total war. As early as 1909 Giulio Douhet, an Italian theorist, wrote: "Any distinction between belligerents and nonbelligerents is no longer admissible today, either in fact or theory. Not in theory because when nations are at war, everyone takes a part in it: the soldier carrying his gun, the woman loading shells in a factory, the farmer growing wheat, the scientist experimenting in his laboratory. Not in fact because nowadays the offensive may reach anyone; and it begins to look as though the safest place may be in the trenches."

During World War I, London had been modestly bombed by Zeppelins and Paris had been within reach of German long-range artillery, but for the most part it remained a front-line war, with minimal atrocities. The only civilians to suffer seriously were those luckless enough to live within the scope of the fighting. The war was fought with patriotism but seldom with the crusading passion that declares the enemy to be monstrous unless he agrees to alter his views on God or politics. During the between-the-wars respite, such passions were building. Soviet Russia had dropped out of the old capitalist European system and saw itself as the champion of universal revolt against the European power arrangements. This threat from the new political Left brought an even more worrisome reaction from the Right, fascism.

Italy's dictator, Mussolini, was the first to proclaim it, in terms that eliminated Rousseau's contractual link between the citizen and his government and treated the state and its people as a single unit, the former taking absolute priority. "Men and women of all Italy! Italians all over the world—beyond the mountains, beyond the seas! Listen! A solemn hour is about to strike in the history of the country. Twenty million Italians are at this moment gathered in the squares of all Italy. It is the greatest demonstration that human history records. Twenty millions! One heart alone! One will alone! One decision!" All this was just another way of saying that, while the citizen was still expected to serve the state, the state no longer owed any obligations to its subjects.

Even as Mussolini's words were applauded, Italian bombers, faithful to Douhet's predictions, were raining down bombs on Ethiopian peasants. These early air raids, minor as they were compared with what would follow, produced outraged world reaction. When the Japanese bombed Nanking, China, in 1937, the United States government stated, "This Government holds the view that any general bombing of an extensive area wherein there resides a large populace engaged in peaceful pursuits is unwarranted and contrary to the principles of law and humanity." The German bombing in the same year of the little Spanish town of Guernica caused as loud a protest and resulted in Picasso's chilling painting of the event, which has since stood as a symbol of man's inhumanity.

One observer remarked about the conflict in Spain, "If this is a civil war, I'd hate to see an uncivil one." Seldom before had such passions been concentrated in a small area. Previewing World War II, Communists and Fascists faced each other. No one was a noncombatant, and priests who opposed the godless Communists from their pulpits were shot by the dozen. Fascists, on the victorious road to Málaga, ran over prisoners with their trucks to save bullets. This was total war for the first time in deed as well as word. Nothing characterizes its perversity more vividly than a nearly forgotten event at the University of Salamanca in 1936. The fighting had just begun, and Fascist General Millan Astray had been invited to speak. Astray's very appearance was a depressing monument to war, which had claimed one arm and one eye and left his body tattooed with fearful scars. His attitude was characterized by the motto *Viva la muerte* ("Long live death"), which he used repeatedly in the course of his speech. The humane old rector of the university, Miguel de Unamuno, felt obliged to counter, "Just now, I heard a death-loving and senseless cry, 'Long live death.' To me it sounds the same as *'Muera la vida'* ['To death with life']." Such observations provoked the general to shout back, *"Muera la inteligencia!"* ("To death with intelligence"), and but for the inconvenience of creating a martyr he might have had the professor shot on the spot. Instead he placed Unamuno under house arrest, where he soon died, officially of natural causes. In terms of world history the incident was insignificant and General Astray is forgotten, but as a warning that men who indeed admire death above life can climb to positions of great power it remains important. A leader of similar corruption was being worshiped by a majority of the German people. Adolf Hitler had already set down his plans of conquest.

World War II

When Hitler launched his attack on Poland, even in Germany the popular fervor that had greeted World War I was lacking. On all sides the memories were too fresh. France, which had furnished the primary killing ground, could scarcely generate a spark of fighting spirit. Yet whereas the First World War had remained largely an imperialist war of European hegemony, the renewed conflict was imbued with far stronger ideological hatreds. As past wars have proven, material objectives never generate the savagery as do those things which touch the spirit. Until World War II, many believed that the Age of Enlightenment had put an end to religious wars in the West. Now they reappeared, disguised as political ideologies. When German Fascist SS troops met fanatical Communists in Russia, the result was a climax of hatred that put the Crusaders' sack of Jerusalem to shame. The depth of depravity was plumbed with the mass extermination of Jews, Communists, and other undesirables in the Nazi death camps. These deeds are today universally deplored, but another aspect of the totality of modern war has been generally and dangerously accepted. That concerns the escalation of aerial attacks on civilian populations.

The 1937 attacks on Guernica and Nanking had been condemned worldwide. When Warsaw was bombed in 1939, President Franklin D. Roosevelt said the German action "has profoundly shocked the conscience of humanity." He characterized the Japanese assault on Pearl Harbor two years later as "a day that shall live in infamy." Similarly, British Prime Minister Winston Churchill branded the German aerial bombardment of Rotterdam as "a new and odious form of attack." In the 1930s the British deputy chief of the Air Staff had stated categorically that no bombs heavier than 500 pounds would be required in the event of war; he was thinking about flattening tanks, not cities.

But by 1943 the advantage had shifted and Roosevelt and Churchill had the long-range bombers. In affirming a policy of saturation bombing, Churchill remarked, "There are no sacrifices we will not make, no lengths of violence to which we will not go." This meant, by 1945, bombs weighing 22,000 pounds and round-the-clock bombing of refugee-packed Dresden; callous headlines in Allied newspapers joked that now all the china in Dresden was broken. There, 135,000 civilians died. The fire bombing of Tokyo claimed another 100,000 civilian lives, presumably in the interest of breaking the people's will to resist. This psychological presumption seems more often to achieve the opposite effect.

Then came August 6, 1945. Germany had collapsed. Japan was hopelessly beaten when an American bomber, carrying out President Truman's decision, released an atomic bomb that killed 80,000 people in forty-three seconds. The pros and cons of doing so will forever be argued. Officially, it was done to save the lives of American soldiers who otherwise would have had to invade Japan. Others insist that the Japanese were about to surrender anyway, that a public demonstration of the atomic bomb on some uninhabited Pacific island would have given them the message, and that its implementation was no more than bureaucratic reluctance to stop a process that involved four years of tremendous effort and countless millions of dollars. Whatever the motivation, total war had been achieved with this new weapon of annihilation. Until the twentieth century the soldier could march away to war satisfied that his sacrifice would help keep the horrors of battle from his home and family. Perhaps the bitterest experience of the Second World War, one not visited upon American soldiers, was to return to find desolation and families who had been subjected to more brutalizing experiences than their own. There will be no fortunate few in the future. As Douhet long ago predicted, the trenches may be the last place of refuge.

That modern war can be waged only with the all-out industrialized effort of a civilian labor force has erased the distinction between combatant and noncombatant. This fact, not an increase in cruelty, has opened the door to total war. Yet perhaps more as consequence than cause, people have come to accept a progressive savagery in modern war—Sherman's fiery march through Georgia in 1865; unrestricted submarine warfare and poison gas in World War I; terror bombing in World War II—and now the great nations live with the proposition that a war of total annihilation is a very real possibility.

The Cold War

World War II was an American success story. It broke down localism in taste and style and strengthened a national consciousness. Part of that consciousness was a sense of world leadership and unparalleled military power. Not long before the war, professional soldiers had dwelt in their secluded garrisons as quiet and alien to policy-making as an order of monks. The war took the military hierarchy, so long distrusted by the civilian side, and turned it into the largest and most expensive feature of government. During the war the President had relied on his generals first and the State Department second for foreign policy advice. Victory did not change all this because it did not bring real peace, but rather the so-called cold-war rivalry between the United States and the Soviet Union for world domination.

It has become fashionable to say that the postwar Soviet menace was a Washington invention, but the often bloodied Russia was a paranoid and fearful giant. While the United States regarded the late 1940s as a time to encourage liberal values and institutions along her own democratic lines, the Soviet Union looked to enlarge her Communist following during the postwar era. Both nations insisted on being "number one." "We shall bury you," promised the Russian leadership. "Better dead than red" became a morbid slogan in the United

States. Ideologically the two states were approaching that dangerous degree of estrangement where each regarded the other as the enemy of the divine.

The situation was unique. Never before had two dominant states competed for world hegemony. The old international balance of several powers had been replaced by a polarized world. In one respect this was hopeful. Whereas the mechanics of world affairs had often seemed subject to fate, as with the bungled diplomacy that had contributed to the outbreak of World War I, now events were less easily attributed to chance and were more directly responsive to human decision.

On the American side, this competition led to President Truman's initiating a policy of containment, which visualized military aid to countries directly threatened by a Communist takeover, economic aid to poor nations where Communist revolution might otherwise prove an attraction, and the building up of military power superior to that of the Soviet Union and its "satellites." The arms race has continued unabated ever since.

Of all the arts of statesmanship, that of compromise has been called the most difficult. The diplomacy of negotiation has never been highly esteemed in the United States or in the Soviet Union. More confidence has been derived from the following syllogism: "Our nation is peace-loving and will not start a war. If we are strong, no one will dare attack us. Therefore peace is assured." To this end a balance of terror has been achieved. Each year half the U.S. federal budget is allocated to this end. Before World War II approximately one worker in a hundred turned out military equipment in the United States; now it is one in every ten. There is an economic price for being militarily strong. One need only contrast the sagging U.S. dollar to the flourishing mark in Germany and the yen in Japan, states whose industries, though flattened by World War II, have had a substantially civilian direction ever since.

Hot War Options

If the balance of nuclear threat were perfect and complete, major wars would be a thing of the past. Unfortunately it is neither, and is no deterrent whatsoever to nations who do not possess nuclear weapons. Whereas the years from 1900 to 1941 produced 24 wars, the years from 1945 to 1975 saw 119, all fought with conventional weapons. Neither the Soviet Union nor the United States has been exempt. While Russia crushed rebellions in Eastern Europe, the United States became involved in the Korean War, called by some "President Truman's Folly," but hailed by others as the salvation of the United Nations and a turning point in the struggle against Communist expansion. If Korea was a qualified success, Vietnam was a failure: ugly, discouraging, and shameful, with our technical superiority shackled by moral reservations that good conscience could not ignore. The 1979 Russian invasion of Afghanistan, a potential first stride toward the oil-rich Persian Gulf, is the most recent threat to world peace. In the long run, such wars are virtually unwinable on the part of a nuclear power, fraught as they are with the very real hazard of bringing the United States and the Soviet Union into nuclear collision.

Some hold that mutual fear of atomic weapons would restrict such a war to conventional weapons. This assumes that one side or the other would accept surrender for the sake of survival. The more likely course seems to be that the side faced with possible defeat would first retaliate with the most deadly weapons in its arsenal. Certainly there are no guarantees that a thermonuclear war would not break out. This is the sad state of mind behind our present balance of terror: the more both sides strive to increase their safety, the more they achieve a sense of insecurity.

It is easy to dismiss the possibilities of an all-out nuclear war. After all, doomsday fanatics have always been marching around with "The End Is Near" signs, yet mankind has never been so well equipped to achieve the apocalypse. The United States, the Soviet Union, Britain, France, China, India, Israel—one after another the scientifically advanced nations of the world have either manufactured, or demonstrated their capability of making, nuclear weapons. And they have so improved these weapons that the capacity to kill and overkill any possible foe has doubled and trebled. We are like soldiers armed with hand grenades, troubled by the fact that, though they can throw the grenades fifty yards, they will create hundred-yard craters. Each nuclear power cradles such a weapon for safety's sake, uneasy in the paradox that, to prevent a war utterly disproportionate to any possible objective, it must stand ready to launch such a conflict. This situation has been labled Mutual Assured Destruction, abbreviated to MAD. Security rests on the proposition that no one will begin the attack if he believes his target, before being obliterated, will return a comparable counterstroke. History contains no record of a permanent balance of power, but thirty years under this "nuclear umbrella" has created a false sense of security or, if not security, acceptance of fate.

This impending doom is so vast that people accept it complacently, preferring to invest their emotions in the local football team and to direct their indignation toward the sexual indiscretions of congressmen. Psychologically the mental attitude is one of denial, like the unacceptance of death's inevitability. This does not make the threat go away. Although no sane government would now directly initiate a program of world conquest, there is always the possibility of unstable leadership— the Hitler or Dr. Strangelove syndrome—and the "fail-safe" hazard of accident, not to mention the escalation of war begun with conventional weapons. The likelihood of outbreak at any given moment because of one of these causes is statistically minuscule, but, given sufficient time, the probabilities multiply to nearly 100 percent certainty.

A nuclear weapons system is enormously complex, and in

every complexity there is a possibility of human or mechanical malfunction. In 1961 a B-52 jet bomber was obliged to jettison a 24-megaton bomb near Goldsboro, North Carolina. Of the six safety catches involved in triggering an explosion 1,800 times more violent than Hiroshima, five failed. There is little solace in observing, "Well, it was only an accident." In the larger sense no nuclear blast is an accident, for the bombs are deliberately built, as are the conditions behind any accident. Without the lethal mechanisms and the bureaucratic hierarchies that run and maintain them, there could be no nuclear wars or accidents.

The possible detonation of nuclear weapons, deliberate or accidental, increases as more countries and individuals know how to make them. In each case there are more fingers on the trigger. These fingers will not always be the steady ones of rational sovereign nations. They may well belong to terrorists and children. In 1970 a letter was delivered to the City Hall of Orlando, Florida. Its typed contents demanded $1 million in cash plus safe-conduct out of the country or the sender would eliminate the city with a hydrogen bomb. To give credence to the threat, a diagram of the bomb was enclosed. The Atomic Energy Commission could not ascertain whether any nuclear material was missing, and when an armament expert decided the device might work, the ransom money was collected. Before it was paid the "mad scientist" was arrested —a fourteen-year-old schoolboy.

Failure of the "National" State?

Humanity, from the beginning of time, has banded together for protection: pack-tribe-city-state-nation, always seeking larger units as smaller ones failed in their purpose. Today, thanks to nuclear technology, not even the most powerful nation can give its citizens security, as the scales have so emphatically become weighted on the side of attack. During World War II it was computed that if one out of ten bombers could be shot down, in the long run the attacks could not prevail, because those who were bombing would be suffering more irrevocably than their targets. In the case of nuclear missiles, however, if one in ten launched gets through, that attack would undoubtedly be regarded as a complete success. In all probability more than one would reach their target, for as defensive systems are improved, their very invention provides the knowledge for modifying attack missiles that can elude them. The result is that the quest for increased military might only continues to diminish national security, and cannot do otherwise.

In short, the national state can no longer protect its citizens against the horrors of total war. Regarded with cold objectivity, the national state has become obsolete in the technical world that science has thrust upon us. Not only is the national state outmoded, with its fierce and limited loyalties, it is an impediment to equitable living and even survival in a shrinking world. All this can be realized intellectually, but to do anything about it—for a nation deliberately to abrogate one ounce of its sovereignty—would be a monumental act. For all the nations of the world to do so would be a miracle.

In 1965 U.S. Secretary of Defense Robert McNamara estimated that a nuclear exchange in defense of national sovereignty would result in 149 million fatalities in the first few minutes. This gives a kind of crazy credence to a senator's remark that if the world were to start all over again with another Adam and Eve, then they ought to be Americans, not Russians. Such sentiments are dangerous since they accept, even anticipate, the necessity of another great war. In so doing they contribute to the historical context in which war is taken as inevitable. If the cold-war balance is maintained indefinitely, that war must finally come, though the victor would command only ruins and the real winners would be those countries farthest from the fringe.

There are some hopeful signs. None of today's nuclear powers glorifies militarism as did the Nazi regime, which was fated to live and die by violence. The world can credit its continued existence to the fact that Hitler predeceased the first atomic bomb by a few months. Today the United States seems chastened by its Vietnam experience. The old Communist dogma that war involving the capitalist countries is fatalistically certain has been modified. China's late Mao Tse-tung described war as "This monster of mutual slaughter among mankind," and the present Soviet and U.S. leadership would concur that total war is no longer a rational instrument of foreign policy. Yet both sides are armed to the teeth. And conflict between the Communist giants, Russia and China, is an ever-present possibility. Not all future leaders may be rational, and there is always the chance of an accident. To counter the statistical doom in this statement, some progress must take place. It is not enough to cry out for the banning of the bomb. Even if every nuclear weapon were dismembered, the knowledge would remain and the bomb would exist as a potential. The only hope is to abolish war as a human institution. To do so would be an unprecedented event in our history, but then the nuclear situation is itself unique. The approach must be positive—not the surrendering of sovereignty, which would be so doggedly resisted, but rather the creation of something new: some extension of law and order that transcends national states to control the heretofore unregulated anarchy that has existed among them. This is not a new idea. It is as old as the first man or woman who looked with horror on the ravages of war and knew there had to be a better way.

TWO

Peacemaking

Blessed are the peacemakers:
for they shall be called
the children of God.

Matthew 5:10

War and violence have been repudiated in as many ways as
they have been endorsed. Very often the basis of pacifism is
religious, although it may be founded on morality or even rational practicality. Sometimes it takes an absolute form, in
which the adherent shuns violence in any form or, for that matter, any activity that supports the violence of others. At the
other extreme, it may be limited along "just war" lines. Pacifism may emanate strictly from the self or take the form of
obedience to the teachings of a leader or the principles of a
community. Some pacifists are content to practice their belief
while others consider themselves world missionaries, propos-
ing plans to encourage peace or at least to ease the friction
that generates war. If war and violence are as old as the human
race, then a vision of peace is as ancient as civilization. Since

the ways of mass slaughter began with the spear and the bow, yielding in time to the machine gun and the thermonuclear bomb, voices of peace have been crying in the wilderness.

Voices in the Wilderness

The first recorded peace lover was the Egyptian pharaoh Akhenaten, who reigned between about 1375 and 1358 B.C. Under the personal title *Living in Truth*, he introduced a new religion of love to ancient Egypt. Akhenaten evidently put an end to human sacrifice and even hunting for pleasure. Unlike pharaohs before and after, he is never portrayed as executioner or victor in battle. Unfortunately his faith died with him, and only in the Far East would similar ideas gain a real following until the time of Christ.

None of these Eastern pacifists were purists, but during the centuries before Christ they did lament the turmoil in ancient China and call into question the ways of the warrior. The first of these writers, about the sixth century B.C., was the Taoist philosopher Lao-tzu, among whose words are: "He who with reason assists the master of mankind will not with arms strengthen the empire. . . . Where armies are quartered briars and thorns grow. . . . Great wars unfailingly are followed by famines. . . . A good man acts resolutely and then stops. He ventures not to take by force. . . . To be elated is to rejoice at the destruction of human life . . . he who rejoices at the destruction of human life is not fit to be entrusted with power in the world."

Closest of all these early Chinese philosophers to Christian pacifism was Mo-tzu, who wrote toward the end of the fifth century B.C.: "The murder of one person is called unrighteous and incurs one death penalty. Following this argument, the murder of ten persons will be ten times as unrighteous and there should be ten death penalties; the murder of a hundred persons will be a hundred times as unrighteous and there should be a hundred death penalties. All the gentlemen of the world know that they should condemn these things, calling them unrighteous, but when it comes to the great unrighteousness of attacking states, they do not know that they should condemn it. On the contrary, they applaud it, calling it righteous."

Although Mo-tzu, who became a minister for the state of Sung, acknowledged a "just war" type of distinction between offensive and defensive wars, the emphasis in his work is upon human equality under a divine being, universal love, and peace.

Another Eastern voice counseling nonviolence was India's Gautama Buddha (circa 563–483 B.C.), who wrote: "Let a man overcome anger by love. Let him overcome evil by God. Let him overcome the greedy by liberality, the liar by truth," and "The sages who injure none and who always control themselves, will go to paradise [Nirvana] where they will suffer no more." Buddha's teaching, which still has millions of followers, so impressed the Emperor Asoka (circa 273–232 B.C.), whose domain stretched from Madras to Afghanistan, that he converted to the faith, honored the sanctity of all life, forbade animal sacrifice, and accepted only religious conquest where war had been before.

The ancient Greeks, for all their enlightenment, produced no serious advocates of peace. Perhaps their passionate civic pride, which made each city-state so internally dynamic, inhibited outward tranquillity. They did make some practical progress toward a body of custom akin to modern international law, which even established agencies for "peaceful settlement" of interstate conflicts. Thoughts of perpetual peace among men, however, were relegated to seven islands of myth, the Isles of the Blessed, or were left to the make-believe women of Aristophanes's play *Lysistrata*, who went on strike for peace. "I'll tell you now," said Lysistrata, "'tis meet ye all should know / O Ladies! Sisters! if we really mean / to make the men make peace, there's but one way. / We must abstain."

The Romans were a martial people achieving an illusion of peace through force of arms, an accomplishment that statesmen since have bloodily failed to emulate. Still Rome had its voices of protest, among them Seneca, who exclaimed: "We are mad, not only individually, but nationally. We check manslaughter and isolate murders; but what of war and the much vaunted crime of slaughtering whole peoples?" Rome was also the fertile field where Christianity flowered with a promise of pacifism it has not yet fulfilled.

Early Christianity

The Old Testament, though ruled over for the most part by a bloodthirsty and partisan God, does have its peaceful prophets. The strict commandment "Thou shalt not kill" has been shown to apply only within the group of chosen people, but there are Micah and Isaiah, who proclaimed: "And he shall judge among the nations, and shall rebuke many people: and they shall beat their swords into plowshares, and their spears into pruning hooks: nation shall not lift up sword against nation, neither shall they learn war any more" (Isaiah 2:4). Eager to implement such teachings were the Essenes, a Jewish sect from the second century B.C., who resolved to harm no one deliberately.

The Bible's real assault on war came with the Gospel according to St. Matthew, reporting Christ's Sermon on the Mount: "Ye have heard that it hath been said, An eye for an eye, and a tooth for a tooth: But I say unto you, That ye resist not evil: but whosoever shall smite thee on thy right cheek, turn to him the other also. And if any man will sue thee at the law, and take away thy coat, let him have thy cloak also" (Matthew 5: 38–40). The Sermon on the Mount has remained the unshakable heart of Christian pacifism, with a strength no doctrine advocating physical force has ever achieved, for it has the power to bind wills indefinitely, while the power that destroys vanishes with its last victim or with the destroyer. Alexander, Napoleon, and Hitler command no followers. Christ and Buddha live on, and men and women still aspire to their visions.

Christian pacifism was in for hard times from the start: first, from imperial Rome, which regarded it as subversive. Christ himself cautioned his people not to swear an oath of allegiance to the Roman state. Rome in its own behalf had recourse to holy writ, particularly Mark 12:17 and the admonition "Render to Caesar the things that are Caesar's, and to God the things that are God's." This did not, of course, overrule the pacifistic gist of the New Testament, and the true Christians remained pacifistic so long as Christianity was not the official state religion. The main point of friction, as it has been for young twentieth-century pacifists, had to do with military service. Church fathers advised against taking the soldier's oath and some, like Maximilian of Theleste (A.D. 274–295), were beheaded as a result. Yet Maximilian's Christian father returned home with thanks to God that he had brought such a present to the Lord.

Less unlucky was St. Martin (circa A.D. 316–397), who was drafted into the Roman army at the age of fifteen and later withdrew as a matter of conscience. To show he did not act from cowardice, Martin pledged to lead the next day's assault, unarmed, into the enemy ranks. That night the barbarian enemies capitulated, and the bloodless victory was attributed to this would-be martyr, who lived on to become Bishop of Tours and found the first monastery in the West.

The first great Christian writer was Quintus Septimius Tertullianus (circa A.D. 160–230). In his *Soldier's Chaplet*, he wrote: "Shall it be held lawful to make an occupation of the sword, when the Lord proclaims that he who uses the sword shall perish by the sword? And shall the son of peace take part in the battle when it does not become him even to sue at law?

And shall he apply the chain, and the prison, and the torture, and the punishment, who is not the avenger even of his own wrongs?"

The change of doctrine began when the Emperor Constantine elevated Christianity from the status of heretical sect to state religion, a deed which, in the opinion of a later Christian pacifist, Leo Tolstoy, poisoned the pure well water of Christian thought and earned the Emperor the title "that canonized scoundrel." Subsequently, with the encroachment of barbarian hordes and the convenient sophistry of the "just war," pacifism vanished as a movement during the Middle Ages.

A few isolated voices survived in such sects as the Albigenses and the Waldenses, followers of Peter Waldo, whose pacifism sprang from the Mosaic law "Thou shalt not kill" coupled with the Sermon on the Mount. Very similar was a fifteenth-century group led by Peter of Chelcic and the Franciscan order of friars who accepted the premise, "Let them not take up the arms of death against anybody or bear such themselves."

Secular voices were also occasionally heard in behalf of world peace. The best remembered was Dante Alighieri, author of *The Divine Comedy*, who about 1310 published his *De Monarchia*, which envisioned one empire governed by one ruler and one universal law. This nostalgia for the lost Holy Roman Empire found little support among the constantly squabbling city-states of Italy. No more popular but at least more forward-looking, toward a kind of world confederation of Christian princes, was *De Recuperatione Terrae Sanctae*, written by the French lawyer Pierre Dubois in 1306. Dubois imagines members of the confederacy using force against any ruler going to war contrary to the principles of the confederation. The modernity of these ideas is rather dimmed in view of the fact that the primary objective of Dubois's writing was to urge yet another Crusade upon the Holy Land.

The Enlightened Peace Lovers

Not until the Renaissance did Western man begin seriously thinking for himself. Until then, God had remained an absolute authority, with rules of conduct based on his express commands, as magically pronounced by the lips of his anointed priests and administered by divinely appointed sovereigns. The Renaissance, which merged into the so-called Age of Enlightenment, nurtured a revival of learning. Religious absolutism yielded grudgingly to rational and scientific thinking. While the Christian pacifists condemned war as sin, those of the Enlightenment called it inhumane and irrational.

Occupying a pivotal position between the two is Desiderius Erasmus (circa 1465–1536). Born in Rotterdam, Erasmus was at age thirteen placed in a monastery by his guardian. Ordained a priest in the year Columbus discovered America, he did not begin his important writings until he was nearly fifty. In 1513 Erasmus wrote to the Abbot of St. Bertin: "[We] . . . who hope for a sublime communion with God, that as Christ and the Father are one, so also we may be one with Him; can any thing in this world be of such value as to provoke us to war? A state so destructive, so hideous, and so base, that even when it is founded on a just cause, it can never be pleasing to a good man."

Erasmus's *Antipolemus (Against War)* came out the following year. "Peace is the mother and nurse of all good things. War suddenly and at once overthroweth, destroyeth, and utterly fordoeth everything that is pleasant and fair, and bringeth in among men a monster of all mischievous things.

"Ye say ye make war for the safeguard of the commonweal; yea, but no way sooner nor more unthriftily may the commonweal perish than by war."

Three years later his *Querela Pacis (The Complaint of Peace)* was published. "As peace, am I not praised by both men and gods as the very source and defender of all good things? What is there of prosperity, of security, or of happiness that cannot be ascribed to me? On the other hand, is not war the destroyer of all things and the very seed of evil? What is there of prosperity that it does not infect? What is secure or pleasant that it does not undermine? No greater enemy of goodness or of religion can be found."

At one point Erasmus suggested that men killed in battle be denied burial in consecrated ground, but then weakened, limiting this punishment to wars between Christians, while opening the old just-war door a bit in regard to what he called "barbarous invasions and defense of the common good."

Erasmus had little intellectual support until writers of the Enlightenment began to flood the market. One of the first to rush into print was a Frenchman, Émeric Crucé, whose work *Le Nouveau Cynée* (*The New Kings*), was published in 1623. Crucé proposed a world union of independent states to encourage the arts, trade, and brotherhood among men. "A Holy Resolve: Great Princes," wrote Crucé, "it is you who must accomplish this holy resolve. Mankind in general and your subjects in particular will be grateful to you. No conquest could win you so much acclaim; no victory deserves so many bonfires. What greater honour can you look for than to see peace proclaimed by your authority throughout the world?"

More influential was *De Jure Belli et Pacis* (*The Rights of War and Peace*), published in 1625. This was the work of Hugo Grotius (1583–1645), a brilliant Dutch jurist and diplomat who practiced law at The Hague. Until this time there had been no rules to curb the barbarity of fighting between Christian states. Shocked by the bloody outrages of the Thirty Years' War, Grotius complained: "I saw prevailing throughout the Christian world a license in making war of which even barbarous nations would have been ashamed, recourse being had to arms for slight reasons or no reason; and, when arms were once taken up, all reverence for divine and human law was thrown away, just as if men were thenceforth authorized to commit all crimes without restraint.''

Remembered as the father of international law, Grotius asserted that sovereignty was not absolute but limited by laws of God, nature, and nations. The actual conduct of states was, for Grotius, the source of the law of nations. All nations had common interests, and in that community lay mankind's great hope. Although war was not eliminated, these writings did have practical impact, as they were a basis for the Treaty of Westphalia, which in 1648 brought an end to the European bloodshed, and more significantly, they helped to remove the shackles of religious dogma from the Western mind, thereby clearing the way for future dictates of reason.

The eighteenth century produced a number of peace plans. Most comprehensive of its time was the Abbé de St. Pierre's *Project to Bring Perpetual Peace in Europe.* Made public in 1712 or 1713, it proposed a senate or sovereign council, with two representatives from each member state, to meet permanently at Utrecht in Holland. Jean Jacques Rousseau breathed new life into this work in 1761 with his *Extrait du Projet de Paix Perpetuelle de M. L'Abbé de Saint-Pierre,* but the thrust of Rousseau's own thought was that, since wars were waged by princes in their own interests, there would be no wars under a republican form of government. As events proved, he could not have been further from the truth.

Two great philosophers, Jeremy Bentham (1748–1832) and Immanuel Kant (1724–1804) rounded out the Age of Enlightenment with their proposals for peace on earth. Bentham's *Principles of International Law,* which included "A Plea for a Universal and Perpetual Peace," came out in 1793. Two years later arrived Kant's *Zum ewigen Frieden (Toward Perpetual Peace),* in which he envisioned a kind of federation of free states. Standing armies would be abolished and reason and logic would achieve a condition of universal hospitality. Both plans made sense on paper, and both were ignored, remembered by history only as a momentary calm before the Napoleonic storm.

The Rebirth of Religious Pacifism

After the Romanizing of Christianity, its pacifism retired to isolated monasteries. With the Renaissance, Christian pacifism enjoyed a lasting resurgence, first with the Mennonites and more importantly with the later Quakers. The Mennonites were a branch of the Anabaptist sect, which had aspired to cut itself off from the life of the state to live like early Christians. "Believing Christians are sheep among wolves, they use neither the worldly sword nor engage in war, since among them taking of human life has ceased entirely," recorded an early Swiss Anabaptist. The later vitality of the movement was thanks to a Dutch Catholic priest and later Anabaptist minister, Menno Simons (1496–1561), who wrote: "Our weapons are not weapons with which cities and countries may be destroyed, walls and gates broken down, and human blood shed in torrents of water. . . . Christ is our fortress; patience our weapon of defense; the word of God our sword . . . and iron and metal spears and swords we leave to those who, alas, regard human blood and swine's blood about alike."

Menno Simon's followers called themselves Mennonites in his honor and do so still. As early as the sixteenth century they were excused from military service in Holland, and as of the eighteenth, in France, but their conscientious objection to violence was not generally well received. Imperial Germany had no room for pacifism, nor did the Soviet Revolution in Russia, where Mennonite communities had prospered under the czars. In fact little survives of their faith in Europe, and Mennonites today are concentrated in the United States and

Canada, where they live apart from the general community, still regarding themselves as sheep among wolves.

More important as a force for peace are the Quakers, or Society of Friends, not only because of their numbers but because, instead of withdrawing, they have long regarded themselves as missionaries for peace in the world. Their founder was an Englishman, George Fox (1624–91), who was jailed in 1654 for refusing to carry a sword in Cromwell's cause. With the Restoration of Charles II, Fox and his followers, after much soul-searching, concluded that war and violence, even when employed by the "saints," ran counter to the inner light of Christ. In January of 1661 they publicly declared to King Charles that they would not take up arms for an earthly kingdom or even in behalf of heaven. Unlike the Mennonites, the Quakers were not content as an outcast minority but felt obliged to carry their message to the peoples of the earth until the realm of saints was achieved. To this end they gravitated to the American colonies, where their greatest success was achieved.

Penn's Holy Experiment

The first Quakers to reach the American colonies were two women missionaries, Ann Austin and Mary Fisher, who landed at Boston on July 11, 1656. New England Quakers, however, soon clustered in Rhode Island, and from the date of its charter, 1663, they dominated the colony until 1714. Rhode Island was never strictly a Quaker community, and the Quakers did reluctantly acquiesce in military measures against those who threatened the external or internal security of the colony, be they Indians, Dutch, or French.

Pennsylvania, on the other hand, was regarded as the "Holy Experiment in the Wilderness," a Quaker Eden. Its charter was granted in 1681 to William Penn, who would write: "Nor is it said the Lamb shall lie down with the Lion, but the Lion shall lie down with the Lamb, that is, War shall yield to Peace, and the Soldier turn Hermit." Such was the theme of the "Lambs' War," but soon after the English Parliament granted religious toleration the Quakers relented in their attempt to conquer the world by the power of the spirit, substituting the objective of sustaining righteousness within the Quaker community.

In the course of the eighteenth century the American Society of Friends would greatly outnumber their English counterpart. Quaker control lasted for seventy-four years in Pennsylvania, but the purity of the Holy Experiment rapidly diffused. A first difficulty was dealing with imperfections within the community. Prisons were reluctantly set up for "redemptive purposes," and many Quakers failed to turn the other cheek when confronted by hostile Indians. One Quaker historian asserted that by the time William Penn returned to England in 1701 the Holy Experiment was nearly forgotten.

Further erosion derived from two primary sources. On the one hand increasing prosperity, particularly in Philadelphia, caused the counting house to rival the meeting house as a center for devotion. On the other hand, there were periodic threats of war with France. Fear of invasion in 1748 encouraged a voluntary militia to muster. With the outbreak of the French and Indian War, Quaker pacifism was confronted by a strong political opposition, and on June 7, 1756, Quaker rule came to an end when the most dedicated Friends resigned from the colonial assembly. As Benjamin Franklin recorded later, "All the stiff rumps except one that would be suspected of opposing the service from religious motives have voluntarily quitted the assembly."

If the Quakers were out of politics, they have never abandoned their antiwar stand. As Anthony Benezet recorded in 1778, "War considered in itself, is the premeditated and determined destruction of human beings, of creatures originally formed after the image of God." Such conscientious objection received its first colonial persecution in 1658, when in Maryland one Richard Keene, refusing to be trained as a soldier, was fined the then enormous sum of six pounds fifteen shillings, and was "abused by the sheriff, who drew his cutlass and therewith made a pass at the breast of the said Richard, and struck him on the shoulders, saying, 'You dog, I could find in my heart to split your brains'" (recorded by Elizabeth Harris, a Quaker missionary).

Pacifism during King Philip's War caused some resentment of the Rhode Island Friends in 1676, and in Pennsylvania, apart from losing political power, it brought a torment of conflicting loyalties during the American Revolution. A few Friends served the English cause, and perhaps one fifth of the adult males of Philadelphia joined the colonial army. The Society of Friends expelled indiscriminately all who bore arms, and one small group of patriotic dissidents set themselves up as the Free Quakers. Only in the southern colonies were Quaker pacifists severely mistreated in their war of conscience, which goes on to this day.

Enlightened European Pacifism

Before the unprecedented slaughter of the Napoleonic Wars, pacifism had been the province of the religious peace sects and the occasional philosopher. Now Europeans began pondering the moral and human implications of technological wars involving masses of humanity. A sense of gloom hung over the Continent, and, more positively, a concern among many that humanity's lot must be improved. This aura of reform embraced the penal system, slavery, temperance, women's rights, and of course war and its avoidance. There were still the Quakers and other religious groups to denounce the sinfulness of violence, and now there was a burgeoning of peace societies, which put their hope in such rational alternatives to war as arbitration of international disputes, treaties, international authorities, the codification of international law, and general disarmament.

These ideas were not new. The Greeks had developed consular and diplomatic procedures. Imperial and Papal ambassadors had been busy throughout the Christian era. There was the Peace of Westphalia to remember. But never before had the ordinary citizen felt entitled to take a hand in international affairs. While Napoleon was still at large, an English preacher, David Brogue, proposed the formation of a peace society. In 1814 a leading English Quaker, William Allen, actually organized one. It was the first of many. The rest of Europe was less enthusiastic, but by the mid-nineteenth century the peace movement had become sufficiently well organized to conduct a series of peace conferences—Brussels in 1848, Paris the following year—at which the famous French writer Victor Hugo (1802–85) argued persuasively for disarmament and proposed a United States of Europe: "A day will come when you, France—you, Russia—you, Italy—you, England—you, Germany—all of you, nations of the Continent, will, without losing your distinctive qualities, and your glorious individuality, be blended into a superior unity, and constitute a European fraternity, just as Normandy, Brittany, Burgundy, Lorraine, Alsace have been blended into France. . . . A day will come when the only battlefield will be the market open to commerce and the mind open to new ideas."

Such peace conferences continued unabated in Vienna, Bern, Antwerp, and Hamburg until the end of the nineteenth century. They were earnest, idealistic, and in the long run ineffectual. Before the century closed, Britain was fighting in South Africa, and World War I was already seen by many as only a matter of time.

Peace Efforts in High Places

The Napoleonic Wars had left the Europe of 1789 in a shambles. Reconstruction was begun with the Congress of Vienna in 1815, attended by the leading statesmen of Europe. From this great coalition against Napoleon emerged the Quadruple Alliance of Austria, Russia, Prussia, and Great Britain. Three years later, a subdued France, under restored Bourbon rule, was included in this Concert of Europe. The result was a landmark in the formation of international organizations. Though born of war, it would continue to enforce the peace with general success and periodic conferences right up until World War I. Unfortunately, its premise was a balance of sovereign power rather than the repudiation of that power as urged by the peace societies.

Other international organizations resulted from this Concert, which, though they did not directly concern themselves with matters of peace and war, did perform mutually beneficial functions implemented through periodic meetings and staff activities. To some extent they preempted a degree of sovereignty, while acting as a buffer in areas of potential friction.

The first of these organizations was established by the Congress of Vienna. It was called the Rhine River Commission, and it had delegates from all nations touching on that river. Its purpose was to provide consistent regulations for commercial Rhine shipping. It was so successful that a Danube River Commission was created in 1856. Other organizations to serve the mutual common interests of sovereign states would follow. In 1875 the Universal Postal Union was established, and it remains today one of the more successful agencies within the United Nations framework. Other such international unions were the Telegraphic Union, the Bureau of Weights and Measures, and the Union for Transport and Railways; none of them directly questioned national sovereignty, but all, within their speciality, supplanted sovereign prerogatives.

The International Red Cross

Of the few nineteenth-century international organizations to survive, the one closest to the heart of war and peace is the Red Cross. Its founder, now all but forgotten, was the Swiss humanitarian Henri Dunant. Like other men of his century, he believed that humanity could uplift itself and that social evils could be corrected, beliefs which have suffered in our century but which must be preserved. Dunant was born in Geneva in 1828 to a prosperous family. His obsession did not seize him until 1859, when he witnessed the battle of Solferino between the Austrians and the French. Stricken by the suffering of the wounded and the scarcity of physicians, he first obtained medical supplies and thereafter lobbied for some international organization to concern itself impartially with war wounded.

In 1864 the first Geneva Convention took place (not to be confused with the Geneva Convention of 1906, which is today associated with establishing those humane rules of war which nations of this century have been at pains to break), and the Red Cross flag, a color reversal of Dunant's native Swiss flag, was adopted. Within two years, twenty nations agreed to its formation. Others would follow. The Red Cross proved itself in the Franco-Prussian War. A war involving Bolivia, Chile, and Peru in 1879 aided the Red Cross in its leap across the Atlantic, but the United States, leery of entangling alliances, still held back.

It took the spunky suffragette Clara Barton to establish the American branch, first as a noninternational society at her home in Dansville, Michigan in 1881. When vast forest fires swept across the state her people were quick to aid the victims. With such a good start, Miss Barton felt confident when she addressed the President and Congress of the United States the following year: "It is my highest and greatest endeavour to wipe from the name of my country the stain of a disgraceful lack of human feeling, and to cleanse it from the reproach of barbarism. I have said that by 1869 twenty-two nations had adhered to the agreement. Now there are thirty-one. For since that time, Romania, Persia, San Salvador, Serbia, Bolivia, Chile, Argentina and Peru have come over. If the United States is fortunate and diligent enough, perhaps it will make the thirty-second on the list of humanity and civilization. If not, it will remain where it is, among the barbarians and heathen."

Her eloquence resulted in a unanimous congressional ratification of the Geneva Convention. The International Red Cross has remained a star of hope in the wars that have raged thereafter.

In 1901 the first Nobel Peace Prize was awarded to Henri Dunant, already nearly a forgotten man, for the "greatest service to international brotherhood." As a curious footnote, the Peace Prize, which has ever since been awarded by the Nobel Foundation, is funded by the vast fortune of Alfred Nobel, ironically an explosives tycoon. In his old age Nobel was won over to the peace movement by his secretary, Bertha von Sultner, whose memoirs were published under the title *Lay Down Your Arms,* in 1889.

Czar Nicholas II

The year 1889 also saw the first World Peace Meeting in Paris. For the next several years, peace conferences were held, usually at The Hague in Holland. After his ascent to the throne of Russia in 1894, the youthful Czar Nicholas II was their chief sponsor. His main concern was the growing burden of armaments. Although the meetings were enthusiastically hailed by all friends of peace, the intransigence of the participants actually quickened the race toward war. Kaiser Wilhelm II of Germany made it known that he preferred his own sharp sword to international courts of arbitration. Nonetheless, the Permanent Court of International Arbitration, however toothless, was created as a result of the Hague Conference of 1899. The Czar kept trying, calling another Hague Conference in 1907, by which time Russia had been militarily thrashed by Japan and had lost most of her motivation for arms reduction.

Peace Through Anarchism

While the kings held their conference and the well-intended middle class attended their peace societies, there was social pressure from below that visualized a world without governments and hence without war. The supporters of this idea of anarchism envisioned means ranging from total violence to the most Christian pacifism. The end result, too perfect perhaps ever to be attained by mere humans, was aspired to by all who claimed to be anarchists. The arguments raised by the more thoughtful anarchists are still important.

Regarded as the patron saint of anarchism was the French politician and journalist Pierre Joseph Proudhon (1809–65). Proudhon had nothing but contempt for the peace strivings he witnessed. In his book *La Guerre et la Paix* (1861) he wrote: "It is not with subscriptions and meetings, with federations, amphictyons, congresses, as the Abbé de St. Pierre believed, that peace can become serious and placed beyond all attacks. The statesmen can do no more than the philosophers: the Holy Alliance has failed; no philanthropic propaganda will achieve anything. Peace signed at the point of the swords is never more than a truce; peace elaborated in a secret meeting of economists and Quakers would make one laugh. . . ."

Yet Proudhon was anxious to put an end to war, and his exasperation was not with peace but with people who failed to comprehend that the capitalistic sovereign state incorporated war within its very nature, and nothing done within its structure would change it. At the heart of the problem, in

Proudhon's opinion, was the inequitable distribution of wealth. As Britain was the wealthiest country, she suffered from the most aggravated maldistribution and was the most prone to war. To correct such a situation, a radical revolution in customs and ideas was necessary.

"What will be the life [of humanity] when it will no longer have a prince to lead it to war, nor priests to assist it in its piety, nor great personages to sustain its admiration, nor scoundrels nor poor to excite its sensibility, nor prostitutes to satiate its luxury, nor buffoons to make it laugh . . .?" Proudhon asks, and his answer is an anarchist's Garden of Eden, made secure by the free human conscience.

The anarchist movement, which flowered after Proudhon's death, had many violent men in its ranks, dedicated to casting down existing institutions forcibly without offering anything concrete to take their place. There were great humanitarians, pacifists as well, who saw much of value in Proudhon's ideas. The greatest mind among them was undoubtedly that of the Russian writer Leo Tolstoy (1828–1910), who had first met Proudhon in Brussels as the latter's *La Guerre et la Paix* was being published. Within the year, Tolstoy embarked on his own towering epic, *War and Peace*. The very title encompasses Tolstoy's preoccupation. At the time of writing he saw Napoleon as a force for evil and those Russians who opposed him as fighters in a just war; yet Tolstoy loathed all war and yearned to explain it away.

On the one hand he saw war as the consequence of man's evil obsession with power, while on the other he felt that war was embodied in the structure of society. In time, Tolstoy achieved a kind of harmony between these seemingly contradictory ideas. Humanity has always readily submitted to the most powerful, shouting over the centuries "The king is dead, long live the king," but in fact Tolstoy felt that in terms of power the king was always dead, for the more power an indi-

vidual has over others the more inevitable and predestined becomes his every action. The king, or emperor, is only a slave
of history, more so in reality than the swarm of humanity he
appears to command. Far from being forced into obedience,
claimed Tolstoy, most people acquiesce eagerly, deriving a
sense of security from sharing a collective group consciousness, which they accept at the price of their own individuality.
So it is that citizen and leader alike serve the nation-state in its
drive for power, the end result of which is collision with other
states, and war. In Tolstoy's view, democracies were no different in this respect. He did not credit their claims of wiser policies when he saw them participating so enthusiastically in the
armament race. Nor did he regard the citizen living under a
democratic government to be free to obey the dictates of his
own conscience. Rather in practice was he obliged to serve the
will of the government, which did not necessarily represent the
individual, simply because he had a minuscule share in chosing
its membership.

To the extent that one's freedoms are limited by governmental dictates man is not free but a servant of the power system.
It was this system Tolstoy was bound to disclaim. He chose
not the path of violent overthrow but that of Christian individ-
ualism. Freedom began and ended with the individual. He accepted literally the perfectionist teachings of the New Testament and angrily denounced Western society in which the
power-hungry sovereign state and war formed an inevitable
equation. When approached by a prospective draftee, Tolstoy
responded, "No matter how dangerous the situation may be of
a man who finds himself in the power of robbers who demand
that he take part in plundering, murder, and rape, a moral person cannot take part. Is not military service the same thing? Is
one not required to agree to the deaths of all those one is com-
manded to kill?" These words have been echoed by conscientious objectors ever since.

Nineteenth-century Pacifism in the United States

The Napoleonic Wars touched American shores but lightly, in terms of the War of 1812, but reform was already in the air. The eighteenth-century Enlightenment had raised hopes that universal peace might be achieved with man's perfection. Many Americans now fervently believed it was the task of the New World to lead in the struggle for universal peace. These were good solid citizens, defenders of the political and social order, so long as it did not encroach upon the rights of private conscience. Their writings, though sincere, are for the most part naïve, simplistic, and Utopian, with a firm foothold in the Scriptures.

Eminent among these individualists was the "Sage of Concord," Ralph Waldo Emerson (1803–82), whose lecture and essay *War* appeared in 1838. Therein Emerson declared: "The cause of peace is not the cause of cowardice. If peace is sought to be defended or preserved for the safety of the luxurious and the timid, it is a sham, and the peace will be base. War is better, and the peace will be broken. If peace is to be maintained, it must be by brave men, who have come up to the same height as the hero, namely, the will to carry their life in their hand, and stake it at any instant for their principle, but who have gone one step beyond the hero, and will not seek another man's life;—men who have, by their intellectual insight or else by their moral elevation, attained such a perception of their own intrinsic worth, that they do not think property or their own body a sufficient good to be saved by such dereliction of principle as treating a man like a sheep. . . ."

The year 1846 brought a sharp outcry from many a Christian conscience at what seemed an unjust war against Mexico. Declaring, "Under a government which imprisons any unjustly, the true place for a just man is also in prison," Henry Thoreau refused to pay taxes which would serve that war and went to jail. At the same time, Adin Ballou (1803–90) published his *Christian Non-Resistance,* which was a first systematic effort to define those terms, together with the prophetic admission "It is a book for the Future, rather than the Present." Another protest was made before Congress in a speech described by some as traitorous, by others as the most fearless statement ever presented to that body. It was delivered by Thomas Corwin, and embodied words such as these: ". . . If I were a Mexican I would tell you, 'Have you not room enough in your own country to bury your dead? If you come into mine, we will greet you with bloody hands, and welcome you to hospitable graves.' . . . But you still say you want room for your people. That has been the plea of every robber chief from Nimrod to the present hour."

Needless to say, the Mexican War went on, but Corwin had enough support to continue his career, becoming Minister to Mexico during the Lincoln administration; President Lincoln had shared his feelings about an unjust war.

The Age of Enlightenment, with its ideas of human perfectability and the participation of the common man in molding his society, prepared the ground for reform in the United States as it did in Britain. Until the War of 1812, conscientious objection was confined to religious sects, particularly the Quakers and Mennonites. Then in 1815 Dr. Noah Worcester formed a Massachusetts Peace Society, and David Low Dodge (1774–1852) organized a similar group in New York. Self-taught and self-made, Dodge had come from a poor Connecticut farm family and prospered as a merchant and elder of the Presbyterian Church. His concern for nonviolence began one night at an inn when he mistook the landlord for a burglar and nearly shot him. From this he concluded it was wrong for Christians to arm themselves with deadly weapons for purposes of self-defense.

Dodge moved on to question the acceptability of defensive war, an attitude he did not make public until the War of 1812 was over. Then he became president of the New York Peace Society and published a small book, *War Inconsistent with the Religion of Jesus Christ.* Not only did he condemn war on Christian grounds but he produced economic and biological arguments as well. War destroyed property, he claimed, thus hurting rich and poor alike, the poor particularly, for it usually fell to their lot to do the fighting. Biologically, it destroyed the flower of humanity, the young and healthy. The elemental ideas propounded by Dodge would for decades remain the most effective American statement of pacifism.

By 1828 there were thirty-six separate peace societies in the United States, most of which on May 8 of that year merged into the American Peace Society, with William Ladd (1778–1841) as acting secretary and editor of its journal, *Harbinger of Peace.* Even at this early stage there was a divergence of views along just-war lines. Some objected only to wars of aggression, concentrating on the limitation of war through arbitration and international law, while more radical pacifists condemned so-called defensive wars as well. The rift solidified in 1838 when William Lloyd Garrison (1805–79) decamped, leading the radical group into the New England Non-Resistance Society. For over twenty years Garrison dominated the New England pacifists, with a creed akin to that of Tolstoy, driven home by the strength of his conviction and personality.

Like Dodge, Garrison rose from poverty to self-made affluence. At age twenty-three he became the editor of a benign temperance newspaper in Boston, *The National Philanthropist,* and through its medium he could declare, "I am not professedly a Quaker, but I heartily, entirely, and practically embrace the doctrines of nonresistance, and am conscientiously opposed to all military exhibitions." Within six months of writing these words, Garrison was in jail, not for his stand against war but because of his passionate declarations calling for the immediate abolition of slavery.

The organized peace movement had never been well received in the South, and those in the North who like Garrison endorsed pacifism found their support of abolition subverting their all-embracing sense of Christian goodwill. Many, in fact, began calling for a holy war against southern slaveholders. When the war came, conscientious objection was left as usual to the Friends and Mennonites. Peace societies collapsed, with only this solace: the war did bring an end to the traffic in human beings. If such deeply ingrained patterns of un-Christian conduct could be eliminated, perhaps the more difficult task of abolishing war was not beyond reach.

The American Civil War had its impact even on the Quakers, particularly the younger members, who felt drawn to participate in what seemed a just cause. Once the Civil War ended, the turmoil subsided, with an evident decline in the Society's interest in the question of peace and war. Even the strict Mennonites found their principles under stress, from younger members of the society as well as the outside community with which it had increasing contact. But if pacifism was shaken within these sects, secular societies espousing the principle collapsed entirely.

Victory and abolition did little to mollify the former champions of peace and goodwill, and harsh treatment of the South was called for. Even Garrison wanted to impeach President Andrew Johnson for the mildness of his Reconstruction program. Pacifism was left to younger men. Garrison's successor was Alfred Love, who formed the Universal Peace Union in 1866.

The national mood toward the end of the nineteenth century was not sympathetic to pacifism. Most Americans shared the expansionist dreams of Teddy Roosevelt, who remarked upon first seeing the Pacific Ocean, "What a splendid place for a big navy!" The public could easily identify with Rudyard Kipling's poem "The White Man's Burden," which extolled the glory of war and the white man's obligation to rule the world (specifically, in the poem, the newly United States–acquired Philippines).

The old American Peace Society re-emerged after the Civil War to continue its restrained campaign for compulsory arbitration between nations and the establishment of an international court of justice, but radical pacifism in America was represented only by Love and his followers. Their Universal Peace Union's program was "to abolish the causes of war, to discountenance all resorts to deadly force between individuals, states, or nations, never acquiescing in present wrongs." The present wrong that Love resisted most valiantly was the Spanish-American War of 1898. With the United States itching to get in on the age of naked imperialism, the powerful and unprincipled newspaper editor William Randolph Hearst sent Frederic Remington to Cuba to photograph the state of war that existed there. Remington wired back that all was quiet, to which Hearst replied, "You furnish the pictures and I'll furnish the war." This piece of cynicism characterized the bullying events that followed. In the United States it was a popular little war. Considerable territory was seized at small cost, and for his moralistic protests Philadelphians burned Love in effigy. Both press and pulpit denounced him. Though this vain fight sapped much of his energy, Love led his group up to the brink of World War I. When he died in 1913, the Universal Peace Union expired with him.

The Twentieth-century Pacifist Spectrum

With the turn of the century, most pacifists envisioned a promising future. Religious wars seemed buried in the past. Conquest for economic gain was no longer profitable under the destructive conditions of modern war. The fierce ideologies that would darken the political skies after 1914 appeared at most to be a small cloud on the horizon. The expression "My Country, Right or Wrong" was being condemned on both sides of the Atlantic by Mark Twain in his essay by that title, in which he denounced the Spanish-American War, using such words as "An inglorious peace is better than a dishonorable war." Denouncing British involvement in the Boer War, evolutionist Herbert Spencer (1820–1903) could declare, "To me, the cry 'our country, right or wrong!' seems detestable" and Ernest Howard Crosby, a disciple of Tolstoy, could publish his scathing antiwar satire, *Captain Junks, Hero,* without attracting much negative attention.

What the peace movement lacked at this time was a sharp focus. At one end of the spectrum were the traditional religious pacifists, for the most part refusing to participate in war. At the other end was a growing body of utilitarian peace lovers putting their faith in the ultimate reasonableness of mankind. Unique to this group was a new phenomenon, the individual war resister, who pledged never to participate in future wars. While Jesus had said, "Resist not evil," this new breed was pledged to resist evil with all his heart and mind. Between these extremes was a vast body of vacillating pacifists who no longer spoke of the "just" war, but allowed for the possibility of "agonized participation" in a war which, if lacking justice, at least might serve to prevent a greater evil. Such men presumed to fight with the awareness of their own guilt as well as the greater guilt of their foes.

The twentieth-century Mennonites generally retained their long-standing dogmatism. As their theologian Donovan E. Smucker declared, "War is sin! War is hell! War is organized atrocity!" When the test came with World War I, the Mennonites proved their conviction by producing a higher percentage of conscientious objectors than any other group.

While many peace associations were declining toward the turn of the century, the Society of Friends (Quakers) was enjoying a renewal, particularly in Britain, where their pacifist doctrine began catching on in the Protestant churches. When war came, they established the Non-Conscription Fellowship (NCF) in aid of conscientious objectors.

This, too, was the era of the business baron turned Christian philanthropist, believing that money could buy anything, even peace on earth. Among these gift givers, Andrew Carnegie stood foremost in his persistent effort to put an end to war. As of 1900, Carnegie regarded himself as a halfway Christian, characterizing his philosophy as "If a man strikes you on the cheek, turn unto him the other also, but if he strikes you on that, go for him." Three years later he was financing a courthouse in The Hague to accommodate a permanent court of arbitration. In 1904 Carnegie denounced war to the tune of $5 million, endowing a fund honoring true heroes—life savers and rescuers—to offset the damaging effect of celebrating killers in uniform. His biggest effort was saved for 1910, when he created the Carnegie Endowment for International Peace of $10 million, the income to be spent to hasten the abolition of international war. Naïvely confident of rapid success, he directed that once universal peace was achieved, the funds be used to eliminate the world's next most degrading evils.

The war, when it came in 1914, nearly broke Carnegie's heart. For a time he despaired, then supported the United States against Germany, recommending with victory that The Hague was the best place for an impartial peace settlement. It might have been a wiser choice than the French palace of Versailles, which became for Germany a symbol of betrayal.

The young science of psychology made its first important contribution to the preservation of peace in the August 1910 issue of *McClure's* magazine, with the publication of William James's theory "The Moral Equivalent of War." This suggestion that those instincts in young men which are receptive to war and violence should not be squelched but channeled into vicarious and socially productive and challenging activities was widely hailed by pacifists at the time. Its psychological validity has since been questioned, but this idea retains adherents. Organizations such as the Peace Corps are a good example of its implementation.

A purely secular institution was the Permanent Court of Arbitration in The Hague. Organized in 1900, it was the culminating hope of a rational age. Three years later, Britain and France agreed that differences of a legal nature, so long as they did not involve third parties or the vital interest of independence or the honor of the contracting parties, would be deferred to this court. Clearly this left many loopholes, but the agreement, however limited, was the first to accept obligatory arbitration. By 1908 the United States approved a similar accord. Despite the great hopes of its promoters, the court was never very busy. Its most famous case occurred in 1910—the North Atlantic Fisheries Case—and successfully sorted out the rights of Canadian and United States fishermen off the Newfoundland coast. If nothing else, the court then established its own feasibility.

Less ambitious but more quietly successful were those international unions which, beginning with the Postal Union, had grown to some thirty public international unions by 1914. These embraced such diverse areas as transportation and communication, labor, public health, the control of opium, and the African slave trade.

At the furthest remove from religious pacifism were the growing political "isms" that foresaw, as their end product, a peaceful world without war or government. Communists and most anarchists anticipated violence as a means to this paradise. Less ambitious, democratic socialism aspired to power via the ballot box. Joining in common cause with the growing labor movement, it became perhaps the single strongest force for peace in a world otherwise primed for war.

Socialism aspired, with some success, to be an international movement and imagined a world brotherhood of working men that would transcend national loyalties. Most socialistic pacifists accepted the Marxist axiom that capitalistic competition made for war, which workers were then obliged to fight; though very much oversimplified, it seemed at the time to make good sense. Nevertheless, when in 1914 war finally came, nationalistic passions brushed aside such occupational ties. Eugene Debs was a lonely voice speaking for the American socialists during World War I when he said, "Our entrance into the European war was instigated by the predatory capitalism of the United States . . . the working class of the United States has no quarrel with the working class of Germany or of any other country."

The Thunder of Guns

The coming of World War I took the peace movement by surprise. The world, having refrained from major conflicts for so long, had been lulled into a belief that the sensible age of peace had arrived. With the first thunder of guns that August of 1914, pacifism was officially silenced in Germany. France banned all pacifist publications, which was hardly necessary since even the peace societies there were infected with the war fever. The stronger British peace societies remained passive, at most working quietly to find an end to the war while giving what assistance they could to the victims and wounded.

It was three years before the United States joined the fray, but during that span the crumbling pacifism of three of its leading citizens may be taken to characterize the disillusionment of the era. The three were William Jennings Bryan (1860–1925), repeated presidential candidate and later Secretary of State;

the celebrated attorney Clarence Darrow (1857–1938); and
Woodrow Wilson (1856–1924), President of the United States.

After visiting Tolstoy at his home at Yasnaya Polyana during
the winter of 1902–3, William Jennings Bryan had announced
his conversion to a Tolstoyan belief in nonresistance. Clarence
Darrow embraced Tolstoy's views at about the same time,
while the idealistic Wilson joined the American Peace Society.
But when war arrived to test their faith, none could sustain it
for long. Darrow was the first to give way; the unprovoked
German invasion of Belgium in 1914 was enough to affront his
legal mind.

The others struggled on. As Wilson's Secretary of State, the
first person connected with the American peace movement to
hold such a post of responsibility for the nation's foreign policy, Bryan lived in torment as the war drew closer. When the
Lusitania was sunk in 1915, Bryan resigned rather than sign a
firm note of protest that he felt might lead to war. Though
elected in 1916 on a peace platform, by the following spring
President Wilson was calling on the Congress for a declaration
of war. His words were deafeningly applauded, though Wilson
still lacked conviction and was reported as saying afterward,
"My message today was a message of death for our young
men. How strange it seems to applaud that." But eventually
Wilson would embrace the great illusion that out of world war
would come world peace. To his credit, he died trying to make
it so. In the end, even Bryan was carried along in support of a
seemingly just war from which a better world would result.
The peace societies, the advocates of international law,
Carnegie's Endowment for International Peace, all had fallen
silent, leaving only the extremes of the pacifist spectrum intact: the Quakers and Mennonites at one end, a few Socialists,
anarchists, and industrial workers at the other.

The last attempt at peace from the center had the air of
comic opera. It involved Rosika Schwimmer, a member of the
Women's Peace Party, and auto maker Henry Ford, whom she

convinced that war was caused by "capitalism, greed, and the dirty hunger of the dollar." To put an end to it all, they decided to take a shipload of pacifists to a projected conference of neutrals. A private steamer, the *Oscar II*, was hired. With Ford exclaiming, "Take away the capitalist and you will sweep war from the earth," the *Oscar II* pulled in its gangplank. Scarcely had it left the dock than one Urban J. Ledoux, referring to himself as "Mr. Zero," plunged into the water after the ship. Dragged kicking from the water, he swore that his only motive in swimming after the ship was to intercept German torpedoes. From then on, the voyage deteriorated from silly to sour. Mrs. Schwimmer lorded it over her fellow passengers, making many enemies. Factions developed. Henry Ford caught cold, retired gloomily to his cabin, and, upon reaching Norway, instantly defected. His fellow passengers who kept the faith were well enough received in Scandinavia, Switzerland, and Holland, but the fight was elsewhere, and it continued with a vengeance.

Conscientious Objection

"It is no time for divided allegiance. It is time for 100 percent Americanism," declared Senator Kenyon of Iowa. This phrase became a popular slogan when the United States entered the war. In such a mood, peace societies, appeals to international courts, all those sane products of the Age of Enlightenment, were swept away for as long as the fighting raged. Only in Great Britain and the United States, the two bastions of the former peace movement, was there something new, the refusal of large numbers of men to be conscripted into military service. They preferred to be punished by the law of the land than to accept the moral condemnation of their own consciences for taking part in organized violence and killing.

Clearly such conscientious objection creates problems for the state. When men elect to set their private moral convictions above the law, that law becomes meaningless, and other men, whose motives may be less commendable, are tempted to follow suit. If a man who declined to kill was willing to serve his government's cause in a noncombative way, he was usually given alternative service. Absolute refusal to take part in the war effort was judged more harshly. In France such men were shot as deserters. Germany locked them up on the grounds of insanity. When Siegfried Sassoon, the embittered English poet, threw away his army medals and denounced the war, he was hospitalized as "temporarily insane," but for the most part Britain tried to deal equitably with this troublesome new breed of pacifist. One reason for this moderation was the fact that conscription did not arrive in Britain until 1916, when two years of disillusioning war had soured the first rush of enthusiastic enlistment. In May 1917, while recovering from wounds, another of England's disenchanted young war poets wrote: "Passivity at any price! Suffer dishonour and disgrace, but never resort to arms. Be bullied, be outraged, be killed; but do not kill." The poet, Wilfred Owen, returned to action and was killed just before the Armistice.

In all, there were some sixteen thousand conscientious objectors registered in Britain during the war. Objectors who felt that the state was entitled to demand some kind of service from its citizens, short of combat, were so employed. Absolutists, who refused to cooperate in any way, particularly when no religious basis for their attitude could be shown, were confined. Among them was the celebrated philosopher and mathematician Bertrand Russell, who declared, "I wish good people were not so mild . . . the non-resistance people I know here are so Sunday-schoolish one feels they don't know the volcanic side of human nature. . . ."

Always a fighter for individual freedom, Russell was by no means an unreserved pacifist. He wrote in *War and Non-Resistance* (1915): "The principle that it is always wrong to employ force against another human being has been held in its extreme form by Quakers and by Tolstoy, but has always been rejected by the great majority of mankind as inconsistent with the existence of civilized society. In this, no doubt, the majority of mankind are in the right. But I think that the occasions where forcible resistance is the best course are much fewer than is generally believed, and that some very great and important advances in civilization might be made if this were more widely recognized. The so-called 'right of self-defense,' in particular, seems to have only a very limited sphere of application, and to be often supported by arguments involving both mistakes as to political questions and a wrong conception of the best type of character."

When the United States entered the war in 1917, with its ideals untarnished, the draft was immediate and there was no chance for sympathy to develop where conscientious objection was concerned. In 1787 James Madison had proposed a constitutional amendment providing for conscientious objection, but it was not adopted. Now, in 1917, those who objected to the war were generally regarded as cowards or enemy sympathizers. Only religious conviction, which in general meant membership in the Mennonite or Quaker sects, was likely to convince the local draft board. Of the 64,693 men who claimed noncombatant status, local boards recognized nearly 37,000 as sincere. Regarded as more trouble than they were worth, only some 20,873 of these qualified objectors were inducted into the Army. Curiously, though all of these possessed a certificate of exemption from combatant service, only 3,989 claimed conscientious objection when the time came to fight. Why? Did it, as with the much decorated Sergeant Alvin York, mean a genuine change of heart?

The few who remained adamant were either given noncombatant tasks or assigned to farm work. Absolute refusal to support the war effort led to confinement in disciplinary barracks (prison) and often harsh treatment. As Bertrand Russell later related in his autobiography, these determined few in the

United States and Britain could at least feel some satisfaction. "When the War was over, I saw that all I had done had been totally useless except to myself. I had not saved a single life or shortened the War by a minute. I had not succeeded in doing anything to diminish the bitterness which caused the Treaty of Versailles. But at any rate I had not been an accomplice in the crime of all the belligerent nations, and for myself I had acquired a new philosophy and a new youth."

The League of Nations

The Great War was followed by the Great Hope: for the first time, world peace would be presided over by a perpetual organization acquiesced in by the bulk of humanity. This was the League of Nations, and its primary function was to prevent another world war. Its chief spokesman at the Paris Peace Conference of 1919 was President Woodrow Wilson: "Wilson the Just," as the worshiping European man in the street called him. Back home in the United States, however, the League was seen as a worldwide extension of Americanism, not the compromising of national sovereignty such an organization demanded if it were to fulfill its goals.

Despite Wilson's efforts to rally support for the League, an exertion that led to his disabling stroke, it was rejected by the Congress, and the United States quickly returned to its prewar mood of isolation from European entanglements.

Though the loss of the United States was a severe blow to the new organization, the League of Nations opened for business in 1920. Supported by the principal European powers, who remained at first united in their foreign policy goals, it was a success throughout the decade. Never was the League's prestige higher than in late 1925 when it settled an encounter between Greece and Bulgaria. A similar Balkan incident had touched off World War I. Now a Greek soldier had been shot down on Bulgarian soil by a frontier guard. Greek Army units were already under orders to advance over the border when Bulgaria successfully appealed to the League.

Eventual disarmament remained the primary objective of those who trusted the League of Nations to maintain world peace. Disarmament, of course, struck at national sovereignty, and so efforts sputtered. By 1930 a draft "Convention on the Reduction and Limitations of Armaments" was finally submitted for governmental approval. In 1932 the International Disarmament Conference began, lifting expectations for perpetual peace. But already the tide had turned.

Greed on the part of the Allies (particularly the Triple Entente—Great Britain, France, and Russia) in exacting staggering reparations from the vanquished (particularly Germany) after the war had created a state of economic stagnation resulting in the worldwide depression of 1929. International relations were embittered. The tendency was to blame national problems on the designs of foreigners, and international cooperation faded in a growing atmosphere of xenophobia. Before the International Disarmament Conference could meet, Japan marched into Manchuria, in 1931. One Japanese poet tried to apologize.

> Again I have become a child of an aching heart
> Carrying the burden of Japan's crime
> Begging the pardon of China and of the world
> With a shattered soul
> I have become a child of sadness.
>   Toyohiko Kagawa

For the most part, however, the Japanese approved of their nation's growing militarism, and eighteen months later Japan quit the League of Nations rather than amend its own policies.

Less obvious but even more serious for the status of world peace were events in Germany, which had never entirely reconciled itself to defeat by the Allies. President Ebert of the new German Republic told German troops, "As you return unconquered from the field of battle, I salute you!" Such statements had led to the widely accepted opinion that the war had been lost by the connivance of the German civilian population, particularly those who made up the new government. Even though a large segment of the German public condemned its political leaders as traitors, the government seemed on the verge of making a success of democracy. The depression, however, which struck nowhere harder, changed all that. Out of its despair rose fascism, with the fanatical Adolf Hitler at its head. Succeeding to power in January 1933, Hitler dragged Germany out of the Disarmament Conference that autumn, and then out of the League of Nations itself. World War II was only a matter of time.

Pacifism Between the World Wars

While the League of Nations had peace as its first objective, it was not a pacifist organization, and though it carried the antiwar hopes of the world, traditional pacifism experienced a rebirth on its own. The climate of the 1920s was favorable. The pacifists were not alone in feeling they had been duped by the wartime leaders, and among them was growing admiration for the absolutists, conscientious objectors who had stood their ground in opposing the all-powerful modern state. Conversely, the fainthearted pacifists who had fallen into step when the bands began to play were at the same time treated with a measure of scorn.

The hope of many postwar pacifists was to achieve the formation of an international movement. Under the name Paco, the Esperanto word for peace, four nations, Britain, the Netherlands, Austria, and Germany, signed up, but beyond this the movement had little success. Slightly better results were achieved within national borders. France was not susceptible to pacifism in its Anglo-Saxon form, but antimilitarism smoldered there, too, particularly among the political Left.

In Russia, Tolstoy's former secretary, Vladimir Chertkov, led the cause of conscientious objection, obtaining a decree of unconditional exemption from military service for its adherents. However, as applications mounted in number, the Russian government became apprehensive. In 1924 the privilege was narrowed to a few pacifist sects, which did not include followers of Tolstoy. Five years later the last pacifist organization, the Tolstoyan Vegetarian Society, was shut down in Moscow, and pacifist activity ended in the Soviet Union.

Anglo-American-style pacifism received considerable attention in both Germany and Austria after the war. It hung on grimly in both countries until 1933, when Hitler's rise to power abruptly ended all pacifist activity.

In the United States, pacifism was once again acceptable. Following a brief postwar resurgence of chauvinism, antiwar novels, plays, and memoirs published by former combatants came into vogue. Pacifist ranks swelled. The most energetic new group named itself the Fellowship of Reconciliation (FOR). Its Protestant core derived its inspiration from the so-called Social Gospel, which aspired to transform human society into a reasonable facsimile of the Kingdom of God, where all men were equal. FOR's primary battleground was the domestic scene, where it felt the seeds of war lay in the exploitation of labor by capitalism. In concentrating on the injustices of domestic society, some members of FOR, without joining sides, regarded themselves as mediators between conflicting groups. Others, who wanted greater involvement, looked to India for inspiration, where Mahatma Gandhi was leading the masses in a nonviolent struggle against the British Empire.

Gandhi: Satyagraha and Salt

No single pacifist has left such a mark upon history as Mohandas Karamchand Gandhi. Civil disobedience may be as old as

Antigone's defiance of Creon in Greek tragedy, but it was left for this frail Indian attorney to take that which formerly had been a matter for the individual conscience and turn it into a mass movement of great power. As a student in London, Gandhi had been impressed by the New Testament, particularly the injunction in the Sermon on the Mount to love one's enemies and not to resist evil by violent means. Removing to South Africa in 1893, Gandhi encountered Thoreau's famous essay on civil disobedience against unjust governmental acts, and with this he organized Indians in South Africa to practice civil disobedience against the racial discrimination encountered there. In 1914 he demonstrated his loyalty to the British Empire by trying to recruit Indian student volunteers to form an ambulance corps for service with the British Army in France. In 1915 Gandhi finally returned to India, taking with him the lessons he had learned, and there applied them for the rest of his life, with results which undid what the East India Company had achieved two centuries before.

The primary principles that guided Gandhi's actions were twofold. The first, called *ahimsa*, was rooted in Buddhism and the Hindu religion. Gandhi took it to mean noninjury to any living creature. The other pillar of his philosophy was *satyagraha*, which translates imperfectly into "nonviolence" or "love force." Neither surrender nor even denial of human conflict, *satyagraha* has been described as a kind of moral and loving jujitsu. When one man attacks another, he expects the victim to flee or fight back, using counterviolence. Gandhi's philosophy denied both these reactions, but like the jujitsu expert the practicer would yield to the weight of the opponent's attack, pulling him on with kindness and love much as the jujitsu expert would derive leverage from his assailant's attack. Morally speaking, this would throw the attacker off guard, resulting, not in a victory for either side, but in enlightened victory for truth itself.

Gandhi's most famous project applying these gestures occurred in 1931 when he protested the British monopoly on
cheap salt, which was needed by the Indian poor. The protest
took the form of a long march through the countryside to
where the salt deposits lay near the sea. The marchers would
not turn back, nor would they respond with violence when the
government moved to stop them. Hundreds were beaten to the
ground, but the march went on. (Had his followers resorted to
violence, Gandhi would have abandoned the protest, as he did
on other occasions.) In this way the salt monopoly was finally
broken. Within less than two decades, by means of the same
principles, Indian independence was restored.

Gandhi's methods have had their critics. Some religious pacifists have claimed that such techniques are akin to war itself
and not the true task of the peacemaker. At the other extreme
are those who say that nonviolence is fine when your foe is
rational, as were the British in India. But what if India had
been invaded by the Nazis? There was much scorn heaped on
Gandhi when he urged the Jews of Europe to respond to
Hitler's legions with nonviolence. It remains an open question.
The war, and the atomic bomb that concluded it, merely solidified Gandhi's beliefs. The fact remains that nonviolent resistance worked for the Norwegians under Nazi occupation, and
later it was a prime force in the struggle for equal rights in the
United States.

Einstein and Freud

The most famous European pacifist of the era was the great
physicist Albert Einstein (1879–1955), who insisted his conviction sprang from so strong an instinct that he believed in taking
a sacred oath never to participate in any act of violence. One
of Einstein's pet theories was that if only 2 percent of the male
population stood firm as conscientious objectors, no govern-

ment would dare start a war with so many men of military age
in jail or refusing to cooperate. As a German Jew, Einstein
could not help but observe the growing threat to world peace in
the early 1930s. With this specifically in mind, he wrote to the
equally famous Austrian psychiatrist Sigmund Freud. Einstein
felt baffled by man's inability to achieve real peace. War
seemed to him to derive from the power cravings of a small
governing class in each state that refused any limitations of
national sovereignty; he also blamed the munitions manufac-
turers. Now, however, he wondered how such relatively small
groups win over the vast public. Domination by prowar groups
of the schools, press, and the Church did not seem answer
enough. Did man have an inherent lust for destruction? Einstein called on Freud for answers, and the psychiatrist labored
to provide them.

Freud indeed believed that the human race was imbued with
an instinct for destruction. He saw in each of us two conflicting
forces: on the one hand, that of love and life, which he called
the *Eros* drive or instinct; on the darker side, the destructive
death instinct, which Freud called the *Thanatos* drive. These
forces he saw locked in eternal conflict, and he was pessimistic
about eliminating the institution of war. In fact, he had no real
psychological solution for Einstein, though he did point out the
twofold requirement for achieving peace among nations. First,
there would have to be a supreme international court to adjudi-
cate differences between states. Second, this court would have
the power to enforce its decisions. The League of Nations fulfilled the first requirement, but the second was sadly lacking.

Presently the Nazi terror would send both geniuses into ex-
ile, the pessimistic Freud to England, Einstein to the United
States, where in disillusionment he would renounce his pacifism very simply. "Conditions, unfortunately, have changed."
Ironically, it was Einstein's scientific contributions—let it be
admitted that the results horrified him—that led directly to the
creation of the atomic bomb.

On the Brink of War

Efforts toward world peace continued unabated. While the years 1840 to 1920 had seen 3,664 international conferences, the twenty years from 1920 to 1940 initiated some 6,568. The majority of these occurred in the 1930s. There were still those who remembered World War I as the war to end wars, and if the conferences came to naught and the League of Nations was hopelessly embroiled in Far Eastern politics, there remained ardent pacifists, numerous perhaps, but without the common focus they enjoyed before the World War.

From the beginning, World War II was a struggle of nearly religious ideologies. Hitler's accession in 1933 raised the threat of anti-Semitism. The Spanish Civil War, beginning in 1936, set Fascist against Communist. While organized labor had been strongly peace-oriented before World War I, the political Left, which now embraced much of the labor movement, regarded fascism as the enemy. In Britain, organized labor endorsed the collective security offered by the League of Nations to the point of favoring attack on Italy when it invaded Abyssinia in 1935. Everywhere, pacifism vanished from the ranks of labor.

In the United States, the Women's International League for Peace and Freedom urged the enactment of a neutrality act, and students, particularly on balmy spring days, left class to strike for peace. "It will take more than flag-waving and bugle calls to empty the colleges for another war," they insisted. Others thumbed their noses at the campus ROTC (Reserve Officers Training Corps) drill squads, misconduct that caused the American Legion to demand a few expulsions. But the war in Spain captured many of these idealists. And Hitler's machinations, so much more obviously evil than any of the blustering blunders that had caused Germany to stumble into World War I, tormented the steadfastness of the most convinced pacifists. When the time came to choose sides, even Bertrand Russell supported his government against a depravity that he deemed greater than organized violence.

Some few pacifists held out, remembering the futility of World War I, and assuming that, if Hitler won the peace, the consequences could be no worse for mankind that if he lost the war. Others gloomily accepted nazism as a unique villainy and fell silent or supported their nation's cause. For the most part, their defeat at Dunkirk galvanized the British as sharply as the attack on Pearl Harbor would electrify the United States eighteen months later. When that time came, only the devout pacifist Jeannette Rankin would vote in Congress against going to war, whereas in 1917, fifty-six members of Congress had voted no. That vote was the end of Miss Rankin's political career, as it was the end of all the organizations, international and private, that had grown up during the between-wars years as an alternative to war. Only the Red Cross persevered, amid the pacifists' criticism that it was working to make bearable that which no man should endure.

Conscientious Objection in World War II

Pacifist groups, religious and otherwise, were silent and isolated during World War II. All they could do was ease the path for conscientious objectors; for this the Friends' Service Committee accepted primary responsibility.

Outside the Anglo-Saxon community, conscientious objectors fared badly. The Soviet Union had long before uprooted all pacifist groups and Nazi Germany imprisoned those who had not fled the country. Most of these were Jehovah's Witnesses. Others, like Dr. Hermann Stöhr, former secretary of the dissolved German section of the Fellowship of Reconciliation, were summarily shot for refusing induction into the German Army.

By contrast, the British response, in a nation fighting for its survival, was a study in moderation. There was wide appreciation there for the individual conscience and the trial it was enduring. As one Quaker theologian wrote regarding his sons, both of military age, "They might feel they had to serve with the Friends' Ambulance Unit or in any relief service Friends might organize; they might feel called to take the absolute position and suffer imprisonment if need be for conscience sake; or they might feel they had to serve with the armed forces. Whatever their decision, they would have my full support. But I told them however they might choose, they would never be entirely happy, and would always have a guilty conscience."

Not only had conscientious objection gained a measure of public understanding and respect from its First World War stand, but those who professed it now mostly did not take the absolutist stand of their predecessors. All agreed that nazism was evil. It was only a question of how that evil could be weighed against the evil of war itself. Most acquiesced this time in noncombative service, and when in 1940 Britain suspended the precious right of habeas corpus, instituting instead Regulation 18B, which allowed those suspected of sympathy with the enemy to be indefinitely imprisoned, it was members of the British Union of Fascists and related groups who were rounded up. Sincere pacifists were not touched, a mark of respect that most conscientious objectors were quick to acknowledge.

The United States experienced a similar moderation of action and reaction on the part of conscientious objectors and government. As did their British counterparts, most pacifists found their choice a difficult one. No antiwar movement was sustained, so pacifism remained at most an expression of private witness. While conscription rose from approximately 3 million in World War I to 13 million, conscientious objectors numbered over sixty thousand, as opposed to some four thousand in the previous war. Among these, 5 percent were uncon-

ditionally registered as conscientious objectors by local draft
boards, 38 percent were given civilian alternative service, and
30 percent were withdrawn from the register.

The real problems arose regarding the so-called humanitarian and selective objectors. The former group could show no
religious background for their belief, professing only that taking part in war was absolutely contrary to their ethical code.
Given much shorter shrift were the rare selective objectors,
who might refuse to fight for or against a particular political
"ism," be it fascism, communism, or capitalism.

In practice, professed conscientious objectors faced three
alternatives as before: noncombatant military service; civilian
service; or jail. The largest group to become noncombatants—
although neither conscientious objectors nor pacifists—were
members of the Seventh Day Adventist Church. They were
perfectly willing to support their government short of taking
human life.

The second alternative was an ambitious program, Civilian
Public Service, which saw some twelve thousand "Conchies"
fighting fires, doing hospital work, toiling on land reclamation
projects. The idea was a good one, but served less satisfacto-
rily in practice since the priorities given such services were
low in contrast to more war-related demands.

The final possibility was prison. A majority of those jailed
were Jehovah's Witnesses, whose claims of being ministers of
God were generally disregarded by the Selective Service
boards. Occasionally these men were treated brutally and
given solitary confinement, more often in military than civilian
prisons, and seldom with the compliance of higher authorities.

The system was not perfect, but it was an improvement; and
when the war was over, conscientious objectors returned to
civilian life without being stigmatized either in the United
States or, more remarkably, in Britain, which had suffered serious bombing and other hardships.

The Bomb

There had been weapons before considered too horrible to use against another human being—firearms in the waning age of chivalry, the dumdum bullet, and poison gas—yet none were seen to bring into question the validity of war itself. Even before the first testing of the atomic bomb, a committee of scientists led by Nobel Prize–winner James Franck, appealed to the United States Secretary of War to permit the bomb to be used only on a barren island because its use against humanity would cause a global wave of revulsion that would outweigh its military accomplishment. Actually, the world took the bomb pretty much in stride. There was numbed horror and a sense of shame on the part of many Americans, but when the nuclear scientist Robert Oppenheimer proclaimed his own sense of guilt to President Harry Truman, Truman is reported to have said to his Secretary of State, "Don't ever bring that man in here again."

Unfortunately, the atomic bomb cannot be so easily dismissed. It remains a potential for annihilation and, as such, brought renewed relevance to the question of pacifism. What had been solely in the province of idealism and religion became now a very practical consideration determining survival. In Japan, at least, the lesson seems to have been learned, and a clause in that nation's postwar Constitution expressly forbids Japanese involvement in or preparation for war. A footnote was added in 1963 with the case of *Shimoda and Others* v. *Japan*, in which five victims of Hiroshima and Nagasaki claimed damages for injuries sustained by the atomic bombs dropped on these cities. The Japanese government objected on the grounds it was not responsible for damages resulting from an act of war. The court held, however, that the bombing was a blind aerial bombardment, contrary to international rules of war at the time, and found for the plaintiffs. The real defen-

dant, of course, was the United States, which by postwar
treaty was exempt from claims by Japanese nationals. Not that
the court meant to shift Japanese responsibility; indeed, it
made a point of rendering its decision on December 7, the anniversary of Japan's attack on Pearl Harbor.

The United Nations

The brightest hope of pacifists and so-called realists seemed to
be the reborn League of Nations. The war had put an end to
what remained of the old European Concert as well as Japan's
short-lived Pacific system which envisioned Japan as the
leader of a close-knit Oriental community of nations. World
power had polarized around the United States and the Soviet
Union, which, even before victory was won, seemed to be
moving toward a system of world order. At the idealistic extreme was the idea of world government. Self-proclaimed realists wanted something less than that, and during the late summer of 1944, at Dumbarton Oaks, the United Nations formally
evolved.

"The work, my friends, is peace; more than an end of this
war—an end to the beginning of all wars; yes, an end, forever,
to this impractical, unrealistic settlement of the differences between governments by the mass killing of peoples. Today . . .
as we go forward toward the greatest contribution that any
generation of human beings can make in this world—the contribution of lasting peace—I ask you to keep up your faith
. . . ." This statement was part of an address to be given by
President Franklin D. Roosevelt on April 13, 1945, in preparation for the San Francisco Conference due to convene later
that month. It was the last speech written by the President, and
it went unspoken since he died on April 12.

At the subsequent meeting, the Allies, now on the verge of
victory, asserted in the United Nations Charter that through

collective security their goal was "to save succeeding generations from the scourge of war." It was twenty-six years since the League of Nations had been born with equal optimism. Unlike the League, the United Nations sought to regulate rather than reduce armaments, with all members agreeing under Article 43 to make available armed forces when required for United Nations use.

The test came on June 25, 1950, when North Koreans stormed over the border into South Korea. On June 25 the United Nations Security Council found under Article 39, Chapter VII, that the act was a breach of the peace and called for withdrawal of North Korean troops. When compliance was not forthcoming, a UN force, led by the United States, undertook what was called a "police action," which in over three bloody years did result in the ejection of the invaders from South Korea. For the first time in history an international organization had undertaken military action on a large scale and prevailed. To that extent the Korean War was a success and a high-water mark for the UN. It was also a very distinct sham, with the United Nations acting less on its own than as a puppet pulled by U.S. strings. With the succeeding enlargement of UN membership, the United States lost its position of monopoly and has reverted to the traditional position of making private arrangements with other powers outside United Nations jurisdiction.

The subsequent history of the United Nations has been one of sad decline, and one for which the UN cannot be blamed. Long before the organization came into formal existence on October 24, 1945, accord between the United States and the Soviet Union was evaporating. Earlier in that year, Soviet Marshal Stalin had sounded a cautionary note at the Yalta Conference. "It is not so difficult to keep unity in time of war since there is a joint aim to defeat the common enemy, which is clear to everyone. The difficult task will come after the war when diverse interests tend to divide the Allies. It is our duty to see that our relations in peacetime are as strong as they have been in war."

U.S. Secretary of State John Foster Dulles was also hedging his bets when he wrote: "We support the United Nations and will not by-pass it in matters within its competence." Since the Korean affair the applied definition of competence has narrowed, and, though probably no ideological camp believes today that its dogma must conquer or perish, none of the major powers are ready to surrender any of their sovereignty into UN hands. Despite notable successes in combatting world poverty and disease, despite a trebling of membership and a tenfold increase in the annual budget, as a keeper of world peace the UN has had little more success than its predecessor and in this respect can offer little solace to its supporters beyond its survival into a middle age which the League of Nations never knew.

If the UN has fallen short of its original peace-keeping promise, if the International Court has heard no more than a case or two per year, the fact that neither has been abandoned indicates that they are still regarded as an important medium of direct communication between nations. The UN thus reduces the likelihood of war breaking out. For many small states in an atomic world it is the one hope for moderating the disputes of the powerful. If nothing else, the UN remains a potential framework to incorporate world government, should mutual trust and confidence among the great states ever increase to a degree where they would mutually surrender sovereignty, at least where armaments and war are concerned. The UN has not failed; only its member nations have.

Pacifism Outside of the United Nations

Pacifism as a distinct movement was at a low ebb after World War II. After all, the UN seemed to have the problem in hand,

and no sooner had this belief come into question than the cold-war era produced a climate unconducive to the flowering of pacifism. In the United States, so-called McCarthyism of the early 1950s branded anything short of flag-flying all-American-ism as subversive, perverted, or communistic. Among the vic-tims of this mentality were the United World Federalists (UWF). The UWF had a predecessor in Andrew Carnegie's 1906 New York Peace Society. Formed during World War II, the UWF's motto was "World Peace Through World Law." They saw the nation-state as no longer serving its purpose. It seemed in his 1946 message to Congress that President Harry S. Truman agreed, when he said, "It requires that we begin now to develop the United Nations Organization as the repre-sentative of the world as one society." A public opinion poll at that time indicated that the American public favored an inter-national police force over national armed forces.

Briefly, the World Federalists rode an incoming tide with their credo: "We believe that peace is not merely the absence of war but the presence of justice, of law, of order—in short, of government and the institutions of government; that world peace can be created and maintained only under world law, universal and strong enough to prevent armed conflict between nations." By 1948 the brief tide had turned. With the USSR proving uncooperative, the United States sought security in NATO (North Atlantic Treaty Organization), which contrib-uted to the widening gap between East and West. By 1950 such groups as "The Dames of the Loyal Legion of the United States of America" were testifying to the subversive character of the UWF and the climate against internationalism was so pervasive that even the UWF fell into step, changed its name to WFUSA (World Federalists of the United States of Amer-ica), and has since accepted the sorry role of stagnation.

It took the incessant test firing of hydrogen bombs in the late

1950s to breathe life back into the otherwise dormant pacifists. The ever-ascendant magnitude of the tests, the occasional fall-out of radiation thousands of miles from the point of impact, could not help but generate a reaction—several reactions, in fact. There was, of course, the path of fatalistic acceptance, the usual human response when a phenomenon takes on a magnitude that bewilders. Even more dangerous was the impractical view of living with the bomb as a reality—that is, making arrangements via "Civil Defense" to defend against thermonuclear attack by digging shelters in the backyard. The third response was outrage against policies that could in any way lead to such eventualities, and this outrage came not only from conscience but hard-headed common sense. A popular analogy to the use of atomic bombs was drawn by the German physician Max von Laue, who hypothesized the dweller in a large apartment house being attacked by burglars. No pacifist, von Laue admitted the right to shoot back, but what if the apartment dweller countered his assailant by blowing up the building? The burglars would have learned their lesson, but the harm done would be greater than anything the apartment dweller could suffer. When asked what he would do if the burglars brought enough explosives to blow up the building, von Laue saw no end being served by the dweller blowing it up first. He would leave it to the burglars to bear the full responsibility for the evil done.

One of the more outraged intellectuals was Bertrand Russell, whose pacifism was one more of practicality than of faith. Russell, who had been a conscientious objector in World War I but supported the anti-Nazi cause in World War II, could not accept the atomic bomb as a legitimate weapon. A weapon, he claimed, is at least a crude means to an end, and must dissolve when the end is achieved, but the hydrogen bomb showed every promise of annihilating the ends. Russell was horrified by the predicted casualties should an all-out atomic war break out: 160 million Americans, 200 million Russians, and all the peoples of Britain and Western Europe, as suggested by a U.S. Defense Department report: "It is true that the threat of war can still be used, but only by a lunatic." Russell commented, "Unfortunately, some people are lunatics, and, not long ago, there were such lunatics in command of a powerful state. We cannot be sure this will not happen again and, if it does, it will produce a disaster compared with which the horrors achieved by Hitler were a flea-bite."

Action followed words. In the spring of 1957, when it became known that Britain planned to test a hydrogen bomb, two Quakers, Sheila and Harold Steele, led a band of pacifists in an attempt to enter the area off Christmas Island in the Pacific Ocean where the test was planned. The effort was of course thwarted and the bomb went off. The following year a boat christened the *Golden Rule* sailed for the U.S. test area around Entiwetok atoll with a Quaker, Albert S. Bigelow, at the helm. It, too, was apprehended and the pacifists taken to Honolulu, tried, and jailed. The participants could not realistically have expected their gesture to close down the bomb testing but, with a nonviolent Christian-Gandhian gesture of self-sacrifice in the name of truth, they succeeded in fueling the fires of discontent about the "Can you top this?" attitudes of the competing nuclear powers.

The year 1957 saw the formation of the first specifically antinuclear-weapons group in the United States, the National Committee for a Sane Nuclear Policy, known as SANE. With spokesmen such as Norman Cousins and Linus Pauling, it argued rationally for an end to nuclear testing. CNVA, the Committee for Non-Violent Action, had the same objective but a more youthful street-protest approach.

In January of 1958, CND, the Campaign for Nuclear Disarmament, was launched vigorously in England. CND's program was summed up by the slogan "Ban the Bomb." Bertrand Russell was among its supporters, and the great humanitarian Albert Schweitzer sent the following radio appeal from Norway:

"At this stage we have the choice of two risks: the one lies in continuing the mad atomic-arms race with its danger of an unavoidable atomic war in the near future; the other in the renunciation of nuclear weapons, and in the hope that the United States and the Soviet Union, and the peoples associated with them, will manage to live in peace. The first holds no hope of a prosperous future; the second does. We must risk the second."

Although CND did by 1962 achieve a limited objective—Britain's unilateral disarmament—the mad race went on, with the Soviet Union testing bombs of twenty-five and over fifty megatons in October of 1961. And still the real crisis was a year away.

The Cuban Missile Crisis

President John Kennedy had said, "Either man must put an end to war, or war will put an end to man." In the autumn of 1962 he gambled on the latter alternative in a week of power-politicking that has been seen by some as a diplomatic master stroke, by others as an unconscionable risking of the future of the human race.

In 1959 a corrupt government in Cuba had been ousted by communism. Two years later, the United States supported an invasion of Cuban exiles trying in turn to throw out the Communists. It failed, and Cuba's ally, the Soviet Union, agreed to furnish Cuba with atomic missiles.

From Kennedy's point of view, Russia was trying to extend its sphere of power into America's backyard, thereby endangering world peace. Seeing this as nuclear blackmail, he refused to back down or grant any concession. He promised military action if the Soviet ships tried to deliver their cargoes of missiles. His luck held, the Soviets backed down, and the liberty of the "free world" was preserved.

There were at that time U.S. missile bases in Turkey, as much within the Soviet sphere of interest as Cuba was within that of the United States. By way of saving face, Russia called for their removal as a condition for withdrawal of the missile sites in Cuba. Despite the fact that the American bases were obsolete, and their unilateral abandonment had already been considered, the United States refused, preferring, it seems, to risk war, and the world lived in fear for nearly a week for the sake of the nation's and the President's self-image.

Perhaps the likelihood of nuclear war resulting was not a great one, but the risk was real, and as such perhaps the greatest gamble for the smallest gain in the annals of the world's history. Some have blamed Kennedy for being irresponsible toward the human race, saying he as much as took Patrick Henry's "Give me liberty or give me death" and perverted it into "Give me liberty or put an end to everything that lives upon this planet," but the responsibility cannot be so easily narrowed. It belongs to all of us who authorize or even passively acquiesce in the establishment of such diabolical machinery.

It is to be hoped that the Cuban missile crisis represents a low ebb in the Cold War, perhaps even a turning point. It must be such if humanity is to survive. In any event, the experience had been a sobering one for both sides. Within the year, with President Kennedy's support, an Atomic Test Ban Treaty, eliminating above-ground testing, was signed by the United States, the Soviet Union, and Great Britain.

Martin Luther King

Independence came to India in 1948, and within six months its prime mover, Mohandas Gandhi, was assassinated by a fanatic. Though Gandhi's nonviolent program struggled on in India under the leadership of Vinoba Bhave, Gandhi's greatest disciple was a black American minister, Martin Luther King, Jr. Besides acknowledging his debt to Gandhi and his concept of *satyagraha* (love force), Dr. King also derived beliefs from

Thoreau and two pacifist professors, Dean Walter Muelder and Allen King Chalmers, both of whom were members of FOR.

The Congress of Racial Equality (CORE) came into being in 1942 as an offshoot of FOR, when it carried out the first sit-in at a segregated Chicago restaurant. But it remained for the inspired leadership of Martin Luther King, Jr., to get the civil rights movement into high gear with the 1956–57 nonviolent boycotting of the segregated buses in Montgomery, Alabama. According to Dr. King, Jesus Christ furnished the motivation and spirit, and Gandhi the method. Together, and with Montgomery as a rallying cry, nonviolent resistance was launched as a mass movement in the United States. Like Gandhi, King succeeded in separating violence from courage. With him, firmness of will without resort to violence was shown to be the purest form of bravery, while lapsing into violence became the sure sign of cowardice.

King was too principled a man to limit his humanitarian concerns pragmatically to the issue of black civil rights. He spoke out too against the war in Vietnam, joining that chorus of protest which to a large extent would shift nonviolent efforts away from civil rights.

The Peace Movement of the Sixties

The war in Vietnam, which preoccupied three American presidents, stemmed from the struggle of Indochina to evict the French. Since the rebels were professedly Communist, the United States regarded the issue as not so much a civil war within national boundaries as a part of communism's design for world hegemony: first Vietnam, then one East Asian country after another, like falling dominoes. So persuasive was this domino theory that it prevailed despite a CIA report indicating that the theory was not in accord with the facts. Even so, first President Kennedy, then Johnson and Nixon poured in supplies, then soldiers. Although the U.S. Constitution allocated to Congress the right to declare war, this was solely a president's war, as Korea had been. There was no declaration. Although the United States insisted that South Vietnam was being invaded from the North, as Korea had been, the contest began as a civil war, and the dubious nature of American involvement was such that President Johnson felt obligated in February 1966 to pressure the American Bar Association into declaring that the war was a legal one.

Legal or not, it was an ugly business, costly in terms of lives and dollars with nothing to show in return, not even glory. The American soldier, fighting far from home in a cause of dubious honor, was hard pressed to justify his presence there, let alone identify a cause worth dying for. As always in wars when the foe is of another race and color, the tendency was to regard the enemy as subhuman, not to be fought or even subdued, but to be exterminated. Atrocities abounded. The United States was becoming known as a bully in world opinion. The American public was increasingly divided in its support of the national war policy, and many in this case felt it was a patriotic duty to hate their country creatively.

Opposition took many forms. Most conspicuous opponents were the young, for it was they who would be obliged to fight in what clearly seemed an unjust war. Their parades and sit-ins followed directly from the civil rights demonstrations and to a large degree sprang from the same sense of morality and an awareness that such nonviolent conduct might change the world. Gandhi and Buddha served as inspirations, more so perhaps than the Christian Church, which was associated with the Establishment and regarded by many as a compromiser on issues of nationally sponsored violence, though priests and ministers were not absent from the cause. Curiously, when priests were apprehended defacing Selective Service records in an effort to disrupt the draft, the public was shocked. Priests were not expected to misbehave in such fashion; yet was the cardinal who blessed the cause and the soldiers who fought for it a better Christian?

A more legalistic, and in some cases self-serving, form of resistance, popularized by Thoreau, was to refuse to pay taxes. The point was to stand witness to the truth as the individual saw it, challenging the war-making power and accepting jail if necessary to preserve one's principles. A most outspoken tax objector was Presbyterian minister Maurice McCracken, who asserted that if one was not compelled to pay public money for the upkeep of bawdy houses, why then should he have to pay taxes for a measurably greater evil, the making of war?

The greatest concentration of resisters focused on the draft. Among them, giving his last strength, was the grand old man of American pacifism, A. J. Muste (1875–1967). A minister of the Reformed Church in America, Muste shifted allegiance to the Quakers in 1918. Not one to work through existing institutions, Muste spoke out with a clear voice against both world wars, against the atomic bomb, and against Vietnam as well. He was never victorious yet never defeated, and his own words might serve as his epitaph: "Precisely in a day when the individual appears to be utterly helpless, to 'have no choice,' when the aim of the 'system' is to convince him that he is helpless as an individual and that the only way to meet regimentation is by regimentation, there is absolutely no hope save in going back to the beginning. The human being, the child of God, must assert his humanity and his sonship again."

Another well-known American who had in fact supported America's participation in the Korean War but who encouraged resistance to military service in Vietnam was Dr. Benjamin Spock. Reaction was not limited to the famous. Families came apart over the issue. When a Yale Divinity School student turned in his draft card to the Department of Justice, his father, a former fighter pilot, threw him out of the house.

A few, like the Quaker Norman Morrison, in emulation of

the Buddhist nuns and monks of South Vietnam who had publicly immolated themselves, took their own lives in protest. Morrison burned himself to death before the Pentagon in Washington. His deed did not go unnoticed in Asia, for his picture presently appeared upon a North Vietnamese postage stamp and may have helped to limit the stereotype of the ugly American.

In the end, the accumulations of these outcries led to the curtailment of the Vietnam War, President Johnson's decision not to seek another term, and President Nixon's campaign resolve to bring the war to a conclusion, something he did not pursue with vigor until after a half-million war protestors marched on Washington in 1969.

Uncounted Vietnamese were dead, along with 50,000 American soldiers, and there was a bill for $150 billion. Nothing had been accomplished—nothing except the lesson itself, and that may be a valuable one. Pacifism had had a victory, and national priorities had shifted. The United States no longer saw itself as policeman of the world, and though the Korean War was followed by a mood of "never again," it is hoped that the Vietnam lesson, in terms of greater restraint in foreign affairs, will be more enduring.

The Seegar Case

One positive consequence of the Vietnam War was the legal extension in the United States of the definition of conscientious objection. In other countries, that status had been broadened as a consequence of World War II. The Scandinavian countries—Denmark, Sweden, Norway, and Finland—granted conscientious-objector status to anyone who could prove his sincerity while at the same time accepting alternative nonmilitary service. West Germany, with a strong reaction against the Nazi era when conscientious objection was a capital crime, enacted a similar provision, substituting civilian service for anyone who opposed, on grounds of conscience, using weapons between states. The United States was slow to follow the trend. At the end of World War II, conscientious objection was available only to those with belief in a Supreme Being, and expressly a Supreme Being who would not condone violence. In 1948 this was broadened as a violation of due process favoring one religion over another. Then in 1965 came the case of Daniel A. Seegar, who claimed to be religious but would not affirm his faith in a Supreme Being. The court held in Seegar's behalf, saying "the test of belief in relation to a 'Supreme Being' is whether a given belief that is sincere and meaningful occupies a place in the life of its possessor parallel to that filled by the orthodox belief in God of one who clearly qualifies for the exemption. Where such beliefs have parallel positions in the lives of their respective holders, we cannot say that one is in relation to a 'Supreme Being' and the other is not."

Pursuant to this decision, when the duration of military service was extended in 1967 the term "Supreme Being" was dropped. As of 1970, in a majority opinion, Justice Hugo L. Black further elaborated, providing exemptions for "all those whose consciences, spurred by deeply held moral, ethical or religious beliefs, would give them no rest or peace if they allowed themselves to become part of an instrument of war." However, the line was drawn when the unwillingness stemmed from political or sociological grounds. It was not granted to "selective" objectors like Bertrand Russell, who might judge one war to be unacceptable and another necessary. So long as the nation-state maintains itself, the possibility that it will allow its citizens freedom to discriminate in this regard seems to be remote.

The Future for Peace

The old pacifist slogan "Wars will end when men refuse to fight" sounds sadly naïve today. Though pacifism may have made gains, the likelihood that it will triumph within the fore-seeable future is more than remote. Yet the realities of this nuclear age demand that adjustments between super-states must be made by other than violent methods. If the United States has begun to see itself as a member of the world commu-nity, rather than its stern guardian, the sense of nationalism has relaxed very little toward real internationalism. The same can be said for other nation-states. Dangerous years lie ahead, and the struggle between those forces pressing for peace and those moving toward war will intensify. The outcome depends on many questions. Is the human animal instinctively violent? Are we killer apes, as some have said? Do we exist within social and political structures which, for their very survival, require war, or at least the menace of war? To predict the fu-ture is a dangerous game, but, as far as the clearer tendencies of the present world are concerned, an important one.

THREE

The Action of the Tiger

In peace there's nothing so becomes a man
As modest stillness and humility;
But when the blast of war blows in our ears,
Then imitate the action of the tiger;
Stiffen the sinews, summon up the blood,
Disguise fair nature with hard-favour'd rage.

Shakespeare
Henry V, Act III, Scene 1

PART I:
Man, the Compassionate Killer Ape

On January 8, 1790, George Washington addressed Congress as follows: "To be prepared for war is one of the most effectual means of preserving peace." The idea was no novelty. The ancient Romans had expressed it in almost the same words, and it has remained a guiding slogan of our own age. A more promising axiom might be: "If you want peace, you must discover why men go to war."

Fighting is common to most species of animals, but few fight to the death, let alone in murderous throngs as do human beings, whose propensity for violence is unmatched by any other creature on earth. History books and the daily news reports are full of cruelties from which we recoil in fascinated horror, fascinated because such bestial impulses lurk in each of us. Yet as the most talented of species, the human race is a paradox, excelling not only in cruelty and murder but in self-sacrifice and compassion, caring even for those wounds inflicted upon its enemies. Mankind, though murdering its Christs, Gandhis, and Martin Luther Kings, multiplies and moves on to greater triumphs of civilization. What herd of buffalo or wildebeest would be so profligate of its great leaders? Yet the buffalo and the wildebeest shrink toward extinction.

In many ways we have rejected violence. Today, prisons, at least in theory, are less for punishment than for reform. The mentally ill are no longer flayed for the demons within them. It is now against the law in Sweden to spank a child. But when war sounds its trumpet, most of us snap to attention still, ready to kill or be killed. Why? The ancient Greeks claimed it was fate. Then Christianity came along and attributed to original sin man's willingness to slay his brother. This served for centuries until the Enlightenment and Jean Jacques Rousseau declared that human nature was inherently good but was inevitably ruined by bad institutions. We are no longer so hopeful that the human being can be perfected.

It is presently fashionable to describe man as bad and to hold that civilization has only provided him with the tools to give wider range to his bestiality. "You can't change human nature" is regularly the explanation for conduct gone astray. It excuses so much, amounts very nearly to a fatalistic full circle. Man is unchangeably bad, so what is the hope for the United Nations or any other institution that tries to make him better?

Aggression

Much depends on whether human nature includes an uncomplicated instinct for aggression—what once was called inherent pugnacity—or whether our tendencies toward violence are a result of the learning process. Charles Darwin in his *Origin of the Species* described the warfare of nature and the survival of the fittest, ideas implying natural aggression that did much to justify Nazi ideas of the master race. The psychiatrist Sigmund Freud seemed to share this pessimistic view of humanity and was quick to flee Nazi Germany. His disciple, Melanie Klein, made a particular study of infant aggression and felt that it existed within the child from the very beginning of life.

The real debate, however, began with recent zoological and anthropological studies initiated by Konrad Lorenz and popularized by Robert Ardrey. For them, aggression is as inherent an instinct as sex and hunger, without which man would not have survived. It is simply a pressure that builds up inside each individual, regardless of outer circumstances, and then periodically must be discharged against some convenient target by way of personal quarrels, fights, crimes, and collectively as riots and war.

Aggression in a constructive sense is seen as that which compels us to overcome obstacles, a kind of life force without which man would not have attained his present world dominance. It is as much a part of achievement as it is of strife. It helps structure society, with the more dominant and successful members rising to the top. Between competing societies, as between competing individuals, aggression develops when both aspire to the same object, presumably the more aggressive being successful. In this way even war has been justified as the survival of the fittest society, and the napalming of children in Vietnam passed off as a sad fact of human biology.

Opponents object that this instinctivistic theory excuses everything from rape to nuclear extinction. Proponents reply on the semantic grounds that aggression must not be confused with violence. If the two were interchangeable, the race would indeed put an end to itself; proponents of aggression, however, see society establishing a variety of rules that curb violence while encouraging aggression. The hope, then, is not of a happy peaceful existence but of a constant precarious sublimation of aggressive instincts short of violence, akin to what William James offered as "the moral equivalent of war," with political machinery being modified as an increasingly adept baffle to violent outbreaks, particularly those with a thermonuclear drift. It is at best a disquieting prospect.

A comparable group, the so-called environmentalists or behaviorists, repudiates the ancestral "killer ape" theory and insists aggression is learned. After all, if Alexander and Napoleon evolved from the heavy-browed club-wielder of the East African savanna, so did Jesus Christ and Mahatma Gandhi. According to the environmentalists, the social situation determines how our genes (whatever their inherent propensities may be) will express themselves. Aggression, like the capacity for speech, is inherent, but the actual ability to speak is learned. Using the anthropological evidence upon which the instinctivists have based most of their findings, they ask why, if we are all descendents of some killer ancestor, are our nearest relatives, the chimpanzees, so relatively peaceful. In fact, why, if we share aggressive instincts with other species, have we turned out to be the most aggressive and violent of animals? While Ardrey and his supporters see aggression stemming from instincts shared with other species, behaviorists believe it derives from differences between us and our animal ancestors. Surely social rules the instinctivists see as a curb on violence actually constitute the abrasive force that make us hyperaggressive.

Behaviorists believe that children learn to be affectionate, submissive, aggressive—whatever—depending on what proves to be the most successful method of getting what they want. If little Jimmy gets what he wants from his mother or younger brother by using force (a temper tantrum with his mother, hitting his brother), then that is how he will act. The behaviorists do not deny that the human being possesses a potential for aggression, but insist that aggression requires an outer stimulus to call it forth. The distinction may seem slight, but whereas the aggressive instinct would require constant frustrating and rechanneling, learned behavior is simply a matter of teaching methods.

The instinctivists argue that aggression has been the guiding force behind social evolution. Their opponents say that, on the contrary, the ability to cooperate has been the test of a successful social group. Without mutual aid, humanity long ago would have been extinct, and this potential to be helpful is as much a human quality as aggression. In shaping human society, even in waging war, cooperation has proved the more vital of the two.

The position of war in this debate is paradoxical. On the one hand, wars would never take place in the absence of aggression and violence. On the other, if aggression was a primary instinct with early man, why did he not wipe himself out? Why, instead, with the growth of civilization has war become increasingly lethal? One anthropologist who repudiated war as the end result of instinctive aggression was Margaret Mead. She took as an example the Eskimo, in whom violent passions are not lacking, but among whom that form of conduct known as war has never been learned.

There are persuasive arguments to the effect that war is not even a very satisfactory outlet for violence and hostility. If it were, and if all men hungered after violence, why do governments require conscription? Individual aggression is sudden, momentary, and usually aimed at a particular individual, whereas the enemy, in terms of war, is remote and impersonal. Decisions to go to war are generally made long before war breaks out, and only then, at "First Blood," do the individual feelings of hostility really become manifest. As several observers have commented, in wartime the private soldier is more sheep than wolf, following rather than attacking. His behavior is far less instinctive than socially directed.

Territorial Imperative

A corollary to the aggression argument involves the question of "territorial imperative." Those who see aggression as an animal instinct hold that many species, including man, have an inherent drive to acquire and defend an exclusive territory. This territory is an area of space—air, water, or earth—which a particular animal—bird, fish, or mammal—or group of animals regards as a preserve from which rival creatures of the same species are to be forcibly excluded. Ideally, territoriality spaces out the habitat so that all receive an adequate portion of the available food. So long as these boundaries are respected, the supposed instinct acts as a peacemaker. When supplies fail or populations expand, trouble is inevitable.

Man, of course, is taken to be a territorial creature. The legendary plight of the man without a country long predates the present debate, and the axiom that a man's home is his castle is older still. If indeed we are territorial at an instinctive level, this fact combines with the present world population explosion to form a dreary prognosis for the future.

However persuasive the arguments in behalf of territoriality may sound, actual studies of territorial behavior in humans and other creatures have raised more questions than they have resolved, and agree only that territoriality is a far more complex study than preliminary statements suggest. Opponents of the concept adamantly deny that most animals are territorial. They also deny that humans are necessarily territorial as a consequence of their animal ancestry. They say that our hunter-gatherer ancestors showed little interest in territory until they took up farming and settled in one place, not before twelve thousand years ago. If this be the case, territoriality is not instinctive but a learned response to a vast spectrum of social, religious, political, and educational factors.

Appeasement and Human Cruelty

Why is man the cruelest of creatures? Again the instinctivists and the behaviorists are at odds. Zoologists know that animals armed with lethal teeth or claws or massive strength have a variety of ceremonial displays and threatening and submissive gestures that usually obviate actual fighting. Humans also use ceremonial displays such as parades of their armies and armaments during peacetime, and athletic contests such as the Olympic Games which are as much displays of nationalism as of individual prowess and skill. Threatening gestures can be seen in political speeches as well as in raised, clenched fists, and bowing and extending the open and weaponless hand are gestures of submission. But when these appeasement gestures fail, creatures lacking a natural means to murder fight as hard as they can, man included.

The Roman proverb *homo homini lupus* ("man is a wolf to man") has remained a most unfair libel of a creature that among his own kind is a decent and gentle citizen. In fact, carnivores rarely kill each other. When they do kill, they kill for food. They do not delight in so doing. They know nothing about inflicting torture upon their victims. The cat that plays with a mouse lacks the mental equipment to identify with the rodent's terror and cannot appreciate the victim's suffering. Man, unfortunately, has that capacity, and though in the average human being the response to another's pain is compassion or at worst curiosity, there are many who derive a sense of superiority from inflicting torment and humiliation. Only humanity seems to be destructive beyond the bounds of defense and the attainment of life's necessities. Nature has no parallel for human brutality, and though few of us indulge in atrocities, few can deny that they harbor vicious impulses which, if vented, would lead to torture, mayhem, and war.

Whether or not one bases aggression on instinct, it takes two forms that are seen to be natural. The first is defensive aggression: the protection of self and what is seen to be important to the self. This is common to all creatures when confronted with danger. Predatory aggression is limited to creatures that live off other species. Known only to man is the malignant form of hostility that delights in inflicting pain and death for its own sake. This form, though common to such men as Hitler and his henchmen, falls into the province of psychiatry, a discipline that will not be discussed here except insofar as its theorizing touches directly upon war itself.

The Psychiatric View of War

Psychoanalysis in its early days characterized war as a periodic discharge of repressed criminal impulses, in which individual fantasies are brought to collective group fruition. This more appropriately defines war among primitive societies than among advanced civilizations.

Each generation of fathers and sons is seen to have its war. Some psychiatrists have called the phenomenon a kind of deferred infanticide, its primary objective being the killing off of younger men, warriors who have come into their own and are seen as a threat to the older generation of statesmen.

More elaborate than this so-called Cronus complex—the father wishing to destroy his son—is the more familiar inversion known as the Oedipus complex, in which the son envies his father his relationship with the mother. The son wants to overthrow and replace his father, even while he loves his father. This ambivalence of feeling toward the male parent creates an unendurable conflict. In order to love the real father, the son must find substitute fathers to hate. The son will then accept the authority of his father and others within his society who fulfill symbolically similar roles—his boss, his commanding officer or king—transferring his hatred outside the community to similar "father figures" in other groups.

Another psychiatric explanation of war has to do with the repression of guilt. Many ethnologists agree that the belief that death is caused by the hostile magic of other tribes is the most common cause of primitive war. Psychologically speaking, this occurs because the individual subconsciously will not accept the feeling of guilt that would accompany accepting responsibility for the death of a loved one or fellow tribesman. Instead of enduring a sense of guilt, he projects blame upon outsiders, who in turn must be punished. In small, primitive wars the danger to the warriors is often minimal, worthwhile in terms of the guilt avoided. Nuclear wars are another matter. No longer is the price of war psychologically worth paying. According to this theory, the hope of human survival depends upon the fact that it is now less costly to endure one's guilt than to project it onto a potential foe who has the capacity for total retaliation.

The Love of Peace and the Lust for War

Peace, however fragile and frequently violated, is taken for granted by most human beings. Never does it elicit the cheerful sacrifices and determined unity of effort expected in war, and yet what sane man would not claim to be a peace lover? War is the enemy of life and liberty and the most wasteful way of resolving human problems. Yet there is much about it that draws the ordinary peace-loving individual, and these appeals, however unfortunate, cannot be denied.

It is no longer considered good taste to characterize oneself as a war lover, but from the sacking of Troy to the fall of Saigon reports are swollen with descriptions of soldiers as wild berserks and heroic killers. Among certain primitive tribesmen, adolescents on the verge of warriorhood spend hours practicing the groans and moans they will make on receiving certain wounds, lest they make a cowardly and unseemly cry when the time comes. German youths preparing for their first great twentieth-century war dwelled upon the so-called Field of Honor where in picturesque death they would prove themselves. The myth of glory and the joy of victory are basic to the American way of life as well. To many there is the unabashed delight in killing, as evidenced in the following letter written home by a young American soldier during World War I:

"All you cheer up and wear a smile for I'm a little hero now I got two (2) of the rascals and finished killing a wounded one with my bayonet that might have gotten well had I not finished him. I'm only going to claim or give my self credit for two that I made hallow [holler] 'mercy comrade mercy.' But I want to tell you I couldn't be satisfied at killing them, how could I have mercy on such low lifed rascals as they are. Why I just couldn't kill them dead enough it didn't seem like. Believe me it was some fun as well as exciting. Now I'm sorry I didn't get to kill one for each of you."

A recent study contrasted the general attitude of Green Beret veterans of Vietnam with young men who resisted serving in that war. A generalization of the typical Green Beret found him to be the son of a strict autocratic father, interested in rough sports and hunting, and without close friendships, male or female. Often a college dropout, he saw himself as a professional who took pride in his expertise. The political and ethical values of the Vietnam situation did not interest him, and it was felt he could easily adjust to fighting for any cause, becoming upset only if he felt he was not adequately discharging his role as a professional soldier.

The war resisters tended to be more introspective, had many friends, kept pets, but did not hunt. Their parents were lenient, at most verbally critical, but not punishers. The war resisters rejected authority figures and ready-made traditional values. In the opinion of those conducting the study, the most significant factor making for divergence between the two groups was their relationship with their parents. In comparing these two extremes with an average group of Vietnam draftees, the scientists found the draftees to be more emotionally similar to the volunteers than to the resisters. However, when the three groups were checked regarding the level of emotional distress caused by the war, both the volunteer Green Berets and the draft resisters proved more composed than the draftees, presumably because they had a clearer commitment to their chosen life-style and regarded themselves, despite hardships, as achieving them. And for the most part it is this unlucky "GI Joe," this puzzled "dogface," who does the bulk of the fighting. What charms has the war to offer him?

Everyman in Battle

War was once the privilege of professionals. With industrialization and the modern state, the privilege of participation was extended to an elite class of young males: first volunteers, then, when these were no longer available, draftees. For the most part these men went willingly enough. "When there was peace, he was for peace. When there was war, he went." He went without any crusading purpose, and for the most part unaware of what he might do to alter the inexorable course of events. He had probably grown up in awe of his government's authority and feeling that, if need be, he should surrender his life according to instructions. This Everyman did not go to war because of a sadistic joy in killing. If he pondered the subject, he might wonder why he was there. Putting aside the national cause and the poetry of righteousness, there is a lure of battle which reaches out to touch most men even though they prefer to deny it.

Combat is hated by the average soldier for the fear and pain and death it brings. The reasons are easily articulated. Yet he loves it, too, often without knowing why. The trumpets of war are said to blow a youthful sound, and the appeal of war is mostly to the young. One need only consider the toys bestowed upon small boys: plastic weapons and model soldiers. Like the games they play, real war to the young is often a grand game in which wounds, if they occur, will be in the left hand— except for the left-handed. As the young poet Alan Seeger wrote to a close friend: "We go up to the attack tomorrow. This will probably be the biggest thing yet. I am glad to be going in the first wave. If you are in this thing at all it is best to be in it to the limit. And this is the supreme experience." It was the last letter Seeger ever wrote.

War as Excitement

If by magic everlasting peace were thrust upon the world, how many groans of regret would mingle with shouts of joy? Many a successful civilian leads a life of quiet desperation, bored, unhappy, disillusioned about his achievements and rewards. War offers a change, other lands, if nothing more the chance of shifting the focus of daily problems. Youths marched off to the American Civil War "to see the elephant," which meant novelty and adventure. Returning veterans, though they may say they hate war, will often admit that they never felt so alive before or since, with the war being "the one great lyric passage in their lives." This may well apply to civilians who see themselves as part of the war effort. A statistic showing that suicide rates dramatically decline during wartime suggests that average life has been given more meaning by the war.

World War I is generally regarded as the most ghastly of wars in terms of combat conditions, but consider the following extracts from two home-bound letters. "From now on expect to have something worthwhile to write about. We leave within 24 hours for the front. Doesn't that sound real thrillin'?" "They are singing and playing cards up there now with their rifles all cleaned and pistols ready. Just simple farmers ready to give whatever sacrifice is asked of them. I shall never be more happy than as a leader of these boys if I am worthy." Boredom is a regular feature of soldiering but never of combat, which subjects the combatant to a whirl of moods—fear, anticipation, longing, doubt, fury, lifting the intensity of simply being alive to an unimaginable height, a "battle high" beyond the capacities of any drug.

The Awe of Battle

Descriptions of religious experiences are usually reserved for biographies of the saints, but the average man is most apt to enjoy equivalent emotions—the awe of being in the presence of or even absorbed by something vastly greater than the self—when witnessing a battle. The grandeur of battle has always cast a spell, inspired poetry. Men lose themselves in its magnificence. If removed from active and terror-filled participation, the observer has a visual feast. In the past it may have been furnished by close-packed crimson-clad regiments, a charge of white horses, the flash of polished brass cannons. To say that war has lost its claim of visual delights is, however, far from true. If removed from the pain and havoc of exploding shells and bombs, the scene remains majestic. Modern war has been visually enhanced by war in the air, preserving a near-religious state of ecstasy that men may never again experience in a life of drab day-to-day existence.

Akin to simply observing the spectacle of massive destruction, there is for many great glee afforded by taking part. What little boy has not derived giddy pleasure from smashing windows or bottles? How much more gratifying is the achievement of a veteran cannoneer or bombardier witnessing their missiles flashing into a target. Any honest soldier would admit that, apart from moral reflections and fears for one's own safety, destruction is a great deal of fun.

Comradeship

War offers a relationship uncommon in civilian life, that of comradeship. This phenomenon must be distinguished from true friendship, which is nurtured in quite the opposite environment of peace. A good friendship is based on love, mutual interests, and the desire to live and do things together. Comradeship depends on shared danger and the willingness to die, not for one's friends, but for one's comrades. Mutual hazard is at the core of comradeship. In combat it is impossible to forget one is in the proximity of crowds who would readily take one's life; without being able to depend on one's comrades-in-arms, this would most certainly happen. The closer to the combat zone, the stronger grows this bond of mutual dependency. Many soldiers who have never before had a true friend find they are surrounded by comrades bound together by the most intense of common goals. This shared purpose in battle is a high point in the lives of many men. Individuals as diverse as Oliver Wendell Holmes and Ernest Hemingway have agreed on this most perfect brotherhood of fellow warriors.

So intense is the sense of sharing with others in combat, this esprit de corps, that a soldier may submerge a sense of his own self in the greater whole. Such group loyalty is the heart of fighting morale. It is the reason for most acts of high courage and self-sacrifice, for when the self has less reality than the group, individual death also to a large extent ceases to exist. Death seems a modest price to pay so long as the group survives and prevails.

The survival of one's group is certainly a stronger motivation for the average soldier than that group's professed objective: the destruction of the enemy. Learning to hate "the enemy" abstractly rarely results in absolute conviction. In reality the devil image is hard to sustain unless, through the loss of a comrade or friend, "the enemy" is transformed into "my enemy." Otherwise the reflective soldier may arrive at the awareness that the common soldiers on both sides are in the same boat, members of one suffering species. If he begins to think in this vein, unless he is sustained by a strong sense of group identification, he will be in trouble.

Apart from the loss of sense of self in combat, other factors combine to make the fighting soldier hold life loosely. The state of mind in battle has often been equated with being drugged. It has been referred to as "battle sleep." The routine and endless repetition of military life contribute to this, as does the state of utter fatigue so common in battle. Historically commanders deprived their men of life's comforts and delights so that the possibility of death might seem as much a source of repose as one of dread. Even when time and energy permit, the average soldier gains little comprehension of the reality of death surrounding him. It is an unreal and alien condition beyond comprehension. The dead seem somehow always to have been dead, a different species, never living creatures like himself. Some soldiers have an unshakable faith in their own survival, a sense of personal destiny, and this belief may well make heroes of them. A religious soldier, if schooled in the tradition of eternal life, may regard physical death but lightly.

Those who lack such faith in self or the hereafter may well be shaken by the violence they encounter, and if they lack as well a sense of common cause and comradeship, they may find combat intolerable. Such a soldier in his emotional isolation may begin to feel that each bullet is aimed at him. Such self-centeredness is at the heart of the most detested of military vices, cowardice. Cowardice has been despised down the ages, perhaps not because such selfishnes is objectionable, but because it threatens the institution of war.

Afterward: Survivorship and Forgetting

Despite war's positive offerings, it seems surprising that more veterans do not look back upon their experiences with horror. Of course, those who have suffered most dreadfully are mute. They are the dead, for the most part transferred so unnaturally and suddenly into this condition that it is hard to believe thereafter that they were even alive. Such deaths quickly become transmuted into hymns, songs, and poetry composed by survivors. The dead never have their say. Seldom do the seriously wounded, who these days are rarely loosed upon the world until they are presentably patched back together. If such patching-up is unacceptable, the mutilated veteran tends to remain in isolation, and when he appears occasionally at Veterans' Day celebrations he is often an embarrassment, even an accusation, to his intact fellows, a symbol of doubt about the merits of the cause for which they had fought. Even among the civilian family of a war casualty the usual response is not to turn to pacifism but to hallow that institution, war, which lends an aura of heroic sacrifice to the memory of the lost loved one.

Not only are war's casualties forgotten or remembered at best poetically, there are great satisfactions in simply being a survivor. Among survivors there is a deep sense of sharing. Differences of status vanish; a sense of comradeship takes over. More than that, there is a profound feeling of superiority to the dead. Even the vanquished have this solace. They are superior to the dead of both sides. Though this satisfaction may be muted by the death of a friend or comrade, the impersonal dead are always in the majority, and as the survivors become that much more exclusive their sense of superiority increases. The survivor is a hero, the annointed of the gods, and scarcely a soldier who has tasted combat will deny this feeling of superiority to a greater or lesser extent. With a few it may virtually become an addiction, so that the peaceful life loses all savor and the survivor must exist within the proximity of other men's dying until he, too, joins them in silence.

Guilt and Dehumanized War

Most soldiers, upon being sworn into service, put great store in the military oath. Once it is taken, they are under orders, and hence blameless for the deeds they are told to perform. In theory this lack of responsibility was denied at the Nuremberg trials after World War II, but in practice, particularly in combat, it is almost unheard of for a soldier to repudiate a command on ethical or humanitarian grounds. If he finds the order repulsive or alien he will probably carry it out nonetheless, feeling himself to be victimized, with little regret left over for the real victim. The retention of guilt is seldom long-lasting, and where it is, the chances are it will become emotionally disabling rather than a positive force acting against future wars.

Vain hope has been placed in the concept that modern war is becoming so horrible that man will lose his taste for it. In fact it is becoming much easier to kill without remorse, even without awareness. Today hand-to-hand combat is the exception. Only the uncommon war lover, gripped by murderous ecstasy, thrives on the proximity of death and mayhem. Now the target is increasingly remote, often not seen at all. The soldier does not kill so much as he serves a machine. He becomes an automaton, manipulating other automatons. The target is no longer a Hun or a gook but an electronic bleep on a screen. Although the end product of the soldier-technician's depressing a given button may be the fiery cremation of thousands, it is far easier to do and to live with than plunging a bayonet into living flesh. That would be a distasteful act for most normal human beings. To pour a can of gasoline over a group of kindergarten children and ignite it would utterly repel all but the most extreme psychopath. Yet place a decent, law-abiding man in a bomber a mile above some target and he will very dutifully release tons of napalm and high explosives, thereby causing excruciating pain and death, without turning a hair.

Even the vocabulary of recent war is deprived of feeling, the horrid realities denied by euphemisms. A village full of peasants is not destroyed, it is "pacified"; a mine made to fly up into the air and explode in a person's face is good-naturedly known as a "bouncing Betty"; a helicopter is simply "hosing" when it fires one hundred bullets a second into masses of writhing people on the ground below. On a larger scale, civilization is seen to exist under the cozy shelter of a "nuclear umbrella," one that is hardly likely to keep out the fatal effects of radiation—and why should it, when strontium 90 is nothing more than a "sunshine unit"?

Now and then guilt does break through, filling soldiers with an anguished doubt. Regardless of orders, these few, when they survive, are not apt to make good soldiers again. Such was the case with one German solider fighting at Stalingrad. His last letter, never delivered, read: "On Tuesday I knocked out two T-34s with my mobile antitank gun. Curiosity had lured them behind our lines. It was grand and impressive. Afterward I drove past the smoking remains. From a hatch there hung a body, head down, his feet caught and his legs burning up to his knees. The body was alive, the mouth moaning. He must have suffered terrible pain. And there was no possibility of freeing him. Even if there had been, he would have died after a few hours of torture. I shot him, and as I did it, the tears ran down my checks. Now I have been crying for three nights about a dead Russian tank driver, whose murderer I am. The corpses of Gumrak shake me and so do many other things which my comrades close their eyes to and set their jaws against. I am afraid I'll never be able to sleep quietly, assuming that I shall ever come back to you, dear ones. My life is a terrible contradiction, a psychological monstrosity."

The individual in war can provide endless speculation and debate. Whether or not the human animal is instinctively aggressive, all that can be said of him is that in the main he can be provoked into fighting in behalf of his group against other groups, but any explanation of the individual in war has no bearing on the question of war itself. The interpretation of war based solely upon personal life must remain inadequate. The individual fights, but he does not wage war. That is exclusively a function of organized groups.

PART II:
The Human Group

The Pack Unit

In *War and Peace,* Tolstoy wrote: "There are two sides to the life of every man: (a) his individual life—which is the more free the more abstract its interests; (b) his elemental swarm-life in which he inevitably obeys laws laid down for him." It is of course this swarm, crowd, pack, tribe, or whatever the term chosen, which goes to war. An odd but once effective test of a war-making community was whether within that group homicide required some form of compensation. Of course, treaties exist now between most nations providing justice between groups, and the only acceptable killings are in certain cases of self-defense or when sanctioned by a state of war. In terms of individual relationships, most civilized men no longer arm themselves. Why, then, do nations refuse to accept a similar high level of conduct? What are the factors that bar this more satisfactory course?

Not all animals exist in large communities, but human beings, with their inadequate natural weapons, found it auspicious to do so when they first prowled the open savannas. They must have conducted themselves much like present-day baboons, who travel with the young and the females flanked on all sides by the most formidable males. Not one alone could hope to match a hungry lion. This pack unit, then, must have been the first real human community or swarm. Today the social unit to which individuals attach themselves has vastly en-

larged into the nation-state. It constitutes the outer ring of loyalties, within which other peaceful units may cluster, down to
the family, and within this structure hostility is controlled by
customs or laws.

Characteristically, each such human community thinks very
highly of itself. Indian tribes often refer to themselves as "the
Men," or "the Human Beings," implying everyone else to be
less in terms of worth and valor. The tribes of Israel regarded
themselves as "the Chosen People," and many nations at one
time or another have concluded that the whole earth is their
promised dominion. Members of these groups tend to internal-
ize their expressed values, values however abstract, for which
they are willing to fight to the death, more readily it seems than
for such concrete goals as food, booty, or land. Typical of such
abstractions was the American "Better dead than Red" motto
of the 1950s, which fortunately has not yet been tested.

In the day-to-day business of living, this larger group identification is seldom tested. Inner loyalties are those which a person has freely chosen—to family, Church, profession. The nation goes on its international way quite independent of its
individual members. They remain for the most part indifferent
and impotent. Questions of foreign policy are generally beyond
their interest or understanding, unless such questions impinge
upon the personal life, as, for instance, when a son is drafted
or events seem to threaten one's home. As long as peace is
maintained, it is easier to identify with one's village or town;
and where hostility is concerned, it is far easier to generate it
toward a neighbor than against a remote nation whose language is strange and whose citizens are unknown. With the
war in Vietnam, the millions of casualties incurred by our ally
South Vietnam never aroused wide concern in the United
States, let alone those endured by the invisible Vietcong, but
as soon as American boys began to fall by the dozen the nation
knew torment.

* * *

Without other human groups to fear, there would be no reason
at all to love one's own group, but the natural response to
strangers is that of suspicion, if not open hostility. At about
eight months of age, anxiety seems to develop spontaneously
within the human child, without any unfavorable experiences
or threats on the part of strangers. The presumption seems to
continue throughout life. There is no more classic tale of individuals being punished for straying from their in-group loyalties to love a member of an alien and hated group than *Romeo
and Juliet;* this hatred is accepted as right and proper. All communities, from ants to humans, reject outsiders and, all
things being equal, close ranks against them. That may make
an end of it, if the strangers retire. Suppose they appear in
their thousands, ignorant, depraved, and morally weak, as
all strangers are supposed to be. At this point a nearly self-
generating process begins to operate within the group that
feels itself threatened. As fear and hatred grow for the out-
sider, bonds of affection and mutual support strengthen
within the offended group. The process is, of course, mutual.
In such relationships two very common psychological phenomena are ready to operate: they go by the names *animism*
and *projection.*

Projection

It is a universal tendency to ascribe all worldly events to some
deliberate human agency. Bad things in life are attributed to
the will of others: neighbors, members of other religious or
ethnic groups, foreigners, Democrats, Republicans, the young,
the old, the rich, the poor. When things in the individual's external environment seem to be going from bad to worse, he
casts about for an explanation. Very often there are spokesmen available who will offer interpretations that are eagerly

grasped, and very often the blame is attributed to the malice of opposing and neighboring groups.

No actual negative intent need exist on the part of the other group. It can be supplied by the phenomenon known as projection. Projection is a very common psychological device whereby one person or group of persons will project feelings of hostility upon another person or group. That is, rather than X admitting he is angry at Y for no good reason, X will conclude that Y is angry at him, and therefore he is entitled to be angry at Y. No tribe or nation wishes to assume the guilt of initiating a war, so it is important to attribute that guilt, by projection if need be, to the enemy. In many primitive societies this is achieved by formalized ritual. Even among the sophisticated Romans there was the rite of the *Feliales*, which charged the prospective foe with guilt, whereby all creation, including gods, humans, animals, and plants, was summoned to bear witness, and a cornel cherry branch—which turned crimson, like blood, on being broken—was thrown into the territory of the future foe.

The process of projection is self-generating and continuously escalating. The outside group becomes the scheming enemy. It is deprived of any good qualities and is quickly stereotyped as "devils," "Commies," or "gooks." Rational discussion and argument are replaced by highly suggestible slogans and symbols. Unless the adversary can to a degree be labeled subhuman, attacking him would to a degree be like attacking oneself. Therefore the exchange of recriminations continues until the image of the enemy—on both sides—becomes cruel, conniving, and vicious. Tension mounts until the members of one group can say with conviction, "They wish to kill us," without adding or even considering the subjective and projected cause, "because we want to kill them." Once this state of righteous arousal has been achieved in a group there is no way to stop the war. Very often the mood has very little correlation with the facts. For example, just after World War II the United States was indisputably the most powerful nation on earth, and yet it felt seriously threatened by the Soviet Union and the majority of Americans questioned by public opinion polls expected war. Today—or until the Russian invasion of Afghanistan, at any rate—the American public is more complacent, despite the fact that Russia has several thermonuclear rockets aimed at every major city in the United States.

Mobilization

War requires more than acquiescence on the part of a group; it requires mobilization. Mobilization, in its simplest terms, is the formation of a belligerent crowd willing to risk all in collision with another crowd. In the nuclear age it is the sovereign state which has monopolized the citizen's private violence. It has often been said that war begins in the minds of men, and the expectation in a people that war is coming must exist. When it does, as with any other threat, be it typhoon or earthquake, distinctions of age, class, and social status tend to vanish for the duration. Short of actual attack by an enemy, mobilization requires a releasing stimulus. When the national leadership is war-minded, it is dependably obliging and will broadcast news of "First Blood" being shed or a provocation by the prospective enemy sufficient to generate fear, anger, and determination among the citizenry. Routines of mobilization are often rehearsed long in advance. Such a ritual with which everyone is familiar is the school fire drill, a ritual which, beyond enhancing the probability of safe evacuation in the event of a fire, establishes a general example of mobilizing a group in the event of an emergency. At the sound of the alarm bell, students give up their diverse activities and fall into a line of march. Organized games and spectator sports furnish similar practice in organizing group activity toward a common goal, usually more or less combative, against some similarly organized group, with nonparticipants organized in support.

Psychological mobilization is rehearsed in the glorification of past wars, with parades, monuments and memorials, the wearing of decorations, and the placing of wreaths on veterans' graves. Where a society is sufficiently well mobilized, very little psychological preparation is necessary. Fear and hatred may be at a minimum and, as World War II so successfully demonstrated, Japan quickly changed from quaint stranger to insidious Oriental foe into today's peace-loving ally.

Once two or more partisan crowds have been mobilized and war has broken out, the preservation of one's own crowd becomes a matter of survival. To reject one's own crowd would amount to rejecting life itself. In collision, the simple goal of each group is to preserve the largest number of living members, while turning the opposing group into as many dead as possible. To this end, partisan histories are rich in descriptions of slaughter and massacre, the refusal to give or accept quarter. None are so revered as those who died fighting to the last, such as the men who perished defending the Alamo. As a result, they remain to this day the prototype of the American hero. For the war to continue, the group must remain intact, and the size of modern fighting groups is such that wars are on the average protracted longer than those of the past, a tendency somewhat moderated by the more lethal capacity of the weapons used. Even when wars have reasonably been lost, the defeated crowd even more passionately resists the pressures toward its disintegration. When the life of the group seems to its members to supersede the sum of their own collective lives, they may well prefer to perish rather than admit the group's destruction.

The Potlatch

Among certain primitive tribes there exists a ritualized phenomenon short of war itself called a potlatch. In a potlatch ceremony, the competing groups ostentatiously match one another in destroying their own valuables. The side which first runs out of destructibles is humiliated and presumably awed and subdued. Breaking one's own toys may seem to be an absurd activity but, if it successfully serves as a war substitute, it has merit. Curiously, there is much about today's arms race that resembles a potlatch, with the major powers straining their economies to produce expensive devices which they hope never to use and which to date have simply become obsolete, serving no purpose other than to swell the self-esteem of the groups involved.

The Nazi Crowd

The most vivid and extreme modern example of a people becoming mobilized into a warring crowd is of the Germans during the 1930s. Not until the nineteenth century were the Germans unified as one people, but, for no other reason than their central position in Europe, they had known many wars and many enemies. Since Frederick the Great, their dominant Prussian community had produced a series of militant leaders who glorified war. As General Helmuth von Moltke remarked, "Perpetual peace is a dream, and not even a beautiful dream. . . . In war man's noblest qualities are developed." Such notions completely swamped the humanist writings of such philosophers as Immanuel Kant. The citizens of Prussia were accustomed to authoritarian government and had no political experience. When a limited right to vote was granted in 1850, it came as a confusing privilege bestowed by Prussian rulers as a gesture of gracious despotism, not the hard-won right of citizenship as was the case in England and France.

Compared to other Western Europeans, the average German remained politically immature, accepting the dictates from above without criticism or even a healthy skepticism. Prophetically, the philosopher Friedrich Wilhelm Nietzsche declared toward the end of the nineteenth century, "The Germans are always so badly deceived because they try to find a deceiver. If only they have a heady wine for the senses, they will put up with bad bread. Intoxication means more to them than nourishment; it is the hook they will always bite on. A popular leader must hold up before them the prospect of conquests and splendor; then he will be believed. They always obey, and will more than obey provided they can get intoxicated in the process."

By 1930 this subservient crowd had been humiliated in a war that also deprived them of their strong authoritarian leadership. Instantly upon defeat in 1918 they were called upon to participate in the true democratic process, an experiment which, despite staggering postwar inflation and the sense that as a crowd they were ringed round by more powerful hostile crowds, nearly worked. Then, in 1929, the worldwide depression came along. The democratic government was helpless. All sense of personal security vanished, and the desperate mood was ripe for the dual phenomena of animism and projection to operate.

Hitler's evil genius was his gift for sensing these fears and frustrations. Though a common man, he knew how to perform as a strong leader, and that was just what the Germans needed. So commonly do a people upon whom political freedom has been suddenly thrust seek out a dictator that the phenomenon has been given a name: the *authoritarian culture lag*. When old authoritarian values have been discredited and replacements seem unobtainable, a disturbed people is particularly susceptible to a prospective leader who seems to have the answers. Since at first Germany was too weak to confront the Allied group that had defeated her in World War I, Hitler found an alien group within Germany itself—the often wealthy and influential but militarily powerless Jews, whom he characterized as satanic parasites. This group he removed and systematically slaughtered while hammering home the Aryan myth of

German blood. He told the Germans that they were superior to other groups that feared, hated, and envied them. Others had been responsible for their sorry lot and must be punished. Where elements of the German community had distinct and sometimes conflicting desires, Hitler still found answers: work for the laboring man, suppression of communism for the wealthy, the future for the young. As soon as he had unified sufficient support at the polls, he set about mobilizing his new German "Folk" community. This took place at all levels, with the military being enlarged, workers and industrialists locked into government contracts they dared not ignore, and the young boys and girls, from their preteen years, inducted into youth corps that led in a direct line to military or supportive services. With the entire country mobilized behind him, Hitler was ready to take on the world, and did, having by that time so alienated the German group from all other groups that they dared not surrender in a lost cause until they were almost destroyed as a fighting force. As the infallible fountainhead of Nazi values, Hitler was trusted to the last. Despite his failure and crimes, no member of this group successfully turned against him. It took the combined weight of the Allied armies to overcome his devoted legions in battle, and it took his own hand to put an end to his life. At this point the entire structure of Nazism, the artificial ties of a false society that he had almost single-handedly fashioned, vanished, along with its evil genius.

If the Nazi story is the extreme example of a human crowd gone berserk, it is also the story of strong leadership, without which that crowd would have been totally without direction.

Crowd Leaders

That human pack or crowd which wages modern war is an artificial entity known as the *sovereign nation*. The sovereign state does not go to war spontaneously but in accordance with decisions made by its leaders, usually one supreme leader (chief/king/president/prime minister) in response to the recommendations of a group of advisers and sometimes with the sanction of a larger body of representatives of the people. President Harry Truman kept a sign on his White House desk: "The Buck Stops Here"; and there are strong arguments attributing the dropping of the atomic bomb on Japan as well as U.S. involvement in the Korean War to his personal decisions. Tolstoy would certainly disagree, as would many others who believe events are overwhelming and that men in high places are swept along by the flow of events.

To suggest that fate is responsible for history is to say that history is the unintended and unpredictable outcome of countless decisions made by uncounted human beings. No one of these decisions is alone instrumental, but taken as a whole they bring about the events that make up history. To accept such a philosophy absolutely is to throw up one's hands, and the fact remains that as more and more power is concentrated in fewer and fewer hands, it becomes irresponsible to say that fate must take the rap. We may all be in it together insofar as enduring the consequences is concerned, but a relative few must be made to assume responsibility for decisions made in high places. There are times in this atomic age when one man draws conclusions of global importance concerning matters of life and death.

The Political Leader

In the late seventeenth century, Doccalini of Loreto wrote: "The desire to govern is a demon which even holy water will not drive out." Edward Gibbon, the English historian, was in agreement when he recorded: "The moral conflict thus engendered is made tolerable by self-deception concerning the true nature of one's real motives, so that ambition for office is disguised under the mask of devotion to the public interest." Per-

sonal fame and power, not public service, are usually behind
the aspiration to leadership, and no modern President wants to
be immortalized as the one who weakened the office. "We are
the number one nation and we are going to stay the number
one nation" was President Lyndon Johnson's candid assessment, and he escalated the war in Vietnam with this in mind.
His predecessor, John Kennedy, was always being reminded
of his boyish inexperience and how the hard-bitten Soviet Premier Khrushchev would dominate him. To what extent was
Kennedy's dangerous stand during the Cuban missile crisis a
matter of self-image? Unfortunately, when factors in decision-
making seem overwhelming, there is always one clear-cut es-
cape, the threat of violence, particularly when the self-de-
clared number one nation deals with the outside world. No
sane President today wants war, but he may not be able to face
the changes necessary to remain at peace.

The purpose of a President once he takes office is to govern.
In his election campaign he has promised to do so, but in fact
he usually presides over a host of conflicting interest groups.
Domestically, he lacks the clout to raise the price of a postage
stamp, and such thorny issues as inflation are almost certain to
prove him powerless. Only as supreme commander in chief,
directing the nation's armed forces upon foreign soil, can he
fully exploit the vast powers of his office. In tribal societies,
the more narrowly the war-making power is held, the more apt
it is to be used. This seems to hold true today. It seems true,
too, that the leader who calls for a firm, even violent, stand
against foreigners is respected even if overruled, whereas a
ruler who is ready to negotiate or bring in the United Nations
gains an unacceptable reputation for softness.

Most well-balanced leaders are concerned with the public
they represent and are aware of a responsibility to their con-
stituency. They want to be loved. Others see, not the human
beings who make up the state, but the state itself. "In the eyes

of those who found empires, men are not men, but tools," said Napoleon. Hitler was another leader who merged the individual and the state with such public phrases as "You are mine, and I am yours. . . . You are Germany, we are Germany." Like Stalin, Hitler would clap when his name was cheered, as though it were external to his person. This narrowing of a leader's focus to the state, or to himself as the personification of the state, approached in Hitler a condition of *solipcism,* wherein only the self seems to exist. Everyone at some time or another has wondered, "What if I'm dreaming all this." Some mentally disturbed people think no other way, and it is a very dangerous state of mind for anyone in a position of power. Unfortunately, too, when a public begins to venerate its leader, as many Germans did in Hitler's case, there seems inevitably to be a correlation between the intensity of that adulation for one's own leader and the degree of hatred turned against other nations.

The Warlords

President, king, or prime minister—all rely on experts in this complicated world. Those most directly responsible for the war-making process are those who command the armed services. Until quite recently, the professional soldier in the United States was but a poor relation among the Washington power elite. With the full flowering of technological global warfare, the military establishment has taken on a permanent cast. Though the Pentagon flourished the motto "Peace Is Our Profession," it is an obvious fact that the vast military complex survives only through the permanent threat of war and the climate of violence ready to be unleashed. "We" are safe, according to Pentagon dogma, only if "we are prepared to fight," and there is no such thing as being overprepared. As long as we are able to do what we say we will do, whether it be morally justified or not, other nations will respect us. As long as they realize their aggression will be intercepted with more massive aggression, they, like the educated rat anticipating the electric shock, will not attack. Just how well this rather simplistic laboratory formula can be generalized to fit the behavior of complex societies has often been questioned.

It would be a strange general indeed who did not first consider international solutions as military ones. Only through winning battles, and preferably wars, can soldiers rise to the pinnacle of power and glory. Presidents Dwight D. Eisenhower, Theodore Roosevelt, Ulysses S. Grant, Andrew Jackson, and George Washington owed the presidency to victories in battle. Soldiering has its more immediate rewards. Erwin Rommel, admired as the Desert Fox even by his foes, knew everything about war except its brutal stupidity. One need only glance at the faithful letters to his wife, Lu, to see how much Rommel loved war. "Everything is wonderful; I am hoarse from giving orders and shouting. . . . How wonderful it's all been." War for the real professional is a splendid game, all the better for besting a formidable foe. American General George Patton's first victory in North Africa was seriously diminished in his eyes when he discovered a lesser general than Rommel had been commanding the German troops. Perhaps the United States' most talented combat commander, Patton made no bones about relishing battle. Having been promoted in 1940, he wrote to a fellow officer: "All that is now needed is a nice juicy war." His 1944 Christmas message might have been written by Joshua before the walls of Jericho:

"Almighty and most merciful Father, we humbly beseech Thee, of Thy great goodness, to restrain these immoderate rains with which we have to contend. Grant us fair weather for Battle. Graciously hearken to us as soldiers who call upon Thee that, armed with Thy power, we may advance from victory to victory, and crush the oppression and wickedness of our enemies, and establish Thy justice among men and nations. Amen."

Patton's enthusiasm would, at least in time of peace, be considered bad form, and present realities render the professional soldier's game approach inappropriate. It would be the rare soldier, however, given his training and possible avenues of fulfillment, who would be of value in the struggle to eliminate war. An exception may have been General Dwight D. Eisenhower, who remarked as President to British Prime Minister Harold Macmillan, "I believe that the people in the long run are going to do more to promote peace than any governments. Indeed, I think that people want peace so much that one of these days governments had better get out of their way and let them have it." Then, as now, both the U.S. and Soviet governments were imbued with the military mystique. President Eisenhower, no left-wing radical, was the first to warn of the growing influence of the "military-industrial complex."

The Military-Industrial Complex

For 1981 the United States military budget is $143 billion. One in every ten workers is employed in its behalf. The U.S. government has always characterized itself as functioning as a balance of powers, an assumption dependent in the past on the vitality of a large and independent middle class. That may have been valid during the progressive era before World War I, but that war, our first really industrial one, blended the business community with Washington politics. The Second World War saw Joint Chiefs of Staff under President Franklin D. Roosevelt rise to a position of power outranking that of the traditional Cabinet secretaries. President Truman preferred the brief, clear foreign policy statements from the Pentagon to the more wordy and equivocal memoranda issued by the State Department. There have been other societies where the military establishment has been more prominent, and countries that spend a higher percentage of their gross national product on the military, but the only industrial societies today where the military establishment is the biggest crag on the political and economic horizon are the Soviet Union and the United States. Other nations are doing their best to keep up. About 20 percent of global industrial production and 75 percent of world trade are of a military nature. Armaments cost the world 40 percent more than education and three times what is spent on public health.

All this spending, of course, is where industry joins the military complex. American industry was once a great scattering of diverse productive units. Aided by the twentieth-century wars, it has become dominated by a few hundred vast corporations. The U.S. government manufactured most of its own armaments in federal arsenals for World War I. At that time, General Motors went on producing automobiles and did only $35 million worth of war work, without expanding its facilities. In World War II, the same company undertook $12 billion in government contracts and after the second month of the war did not produce a solitary automobile. Whereas former businessmen such as the pacifistic Andrew Carnegie and Henry Ford had looked askance at the military, through the years of World War II American business and the military worked together as an effective and profitable partnership, an arrangement that has persisted ever since.

Preparing for war, even when there is no war, keeps the military strong and many a big business corporation rich, creating a climate in no way compatible with an atmosphere of peace.

The governmental maelstrom known as the military-industrial complex has pulled other parts of the society into its vortex. Business and labor were once seen as hostile competitors, but World War II taught them to work well together. Many workers know that their own livelihoods depend on military contracts. During the years of rising dissent over the Vietnam

War, California defense plant workers wore buttons reading "Don't Knock the War That Feeds You!" Clearly, disarmament is not in the immediate interest of such workers, nor is it encouraged by the scientific community.

World War II began what has been called a love affair between government and the academic world, which saw nazism as opposed to everything it held sacred. Government, with the advanced technology of modern war, needed all the scientific brains it could get. During World War I an army officer had declined offers of help from the National Academy of Sciences because "the Army has a chemist." By 1944 the best minds available were concentrating on development of atomic bombs and, where science went, morality was not always sure to follow. As the leading physicist Enrico Fermi remarked to questioners, "Don't bother me with your conscientious scruples. After all, the thing's superb physics."

Cold-war weaponry has grown steadily more complex, and just as steadily the scientific community has been absorbed into the military-industrial complex. Weapons development is at the center of almost all technology, and such research and development, "R and D" as it is called, absorbs billions of dollars. The program to put man on the moon was spectacular, costly, prestigious in potential military terms, but did virtually nothing to relieve the suffering and privation of mankind. Still, the cost of running universities goes up. They struggle to survive, and when government money is offered for the exploration of military or related projects, it is hard to resist. If our scientists are not entirely a part of the military-industrial complex, they certainly are very much in its employ.

A War System?

The anticipation of war is a basic principle behind all modern states, and the successful prosecution of war has produced many lasting civilizations, including the most prominent ones today. Intellects as divergent as the anarchist Mikhail Bakunin and the psychiatrist Sigmund Freud have attributed to the state a monopoly on murder and mayhem, wherein its citizens are honored and esteemed for engaging in conduct in the state's behalf that otherwise would be punished with execution or imprisonment.

Theorists of a more economic slant have particularly attributed to the capitalist economy, and the voracious business creed that it represents, a drift toward war. Stated simply, capitalism requires constant economic growth, which means expansion abroad, and with economic expansion goes the military presence to ensure the business interests. This is basic capitalist imperialism, and in the Communist view it inevitably leads to war. To end war, Communists say, capitalism must be overthrown and then, in a sort of socialist paradise, war will vanish. This faith, of course, is naïve and totally overlooks the facts of human history. Wars were fought long before anyone dreamed of capitalism and most probably will be fought long after it has gone. But that is not to exclude the imperialistic aspect of capitalism from the causes of war.

To the extent that we have capitalistic imperialism, it has certainly evolved in complexity from the old gunboat diplomacy of the nineteenth century. The important question is, what is the function of business in determining U.S. foreign policy? Does our late twentieth-century version of capitalism lead to war? It used to be said that what was right for General Motors was right for the United States, and clearly the domestic economy depends on overseas expansion. Corporate strength depends on the control of critical resources, and in terms of what is available the United States is rapidly becoming a have-not nation. No nation has ever been so self-indulgent. While comprising but 6 percent of the world population, Americans expend half of the resources consumed annually. Many of these no longer are abundantly available within U.S. borders. Thus far these shortages have been expressed in skyrocketing costs. Before long, if money fails to buy the good life, will force be the only recourse? In the past, American businessmen have obtained special privileges from weaker nations. Clearly it was better for business if this exploitation could be accomplished peaceably. War, at best, is an unsettling and risky venture. Until nationalism recently became a force to reckon with in the underdeveloped world, the U.S. State Department was quick to intervene with strong-arm methods in behalf of American corporations aggrieved by their treatment in other countries. Today a weak government imperiled by revolutionaries, such as Guatemala, will look favorably upon the interests of American corporations, so long as the United States reciprocates with an aid program heavily larded with weaponry to hold off the resident guerrillas. But what impact has the business community when issues threatening world peace are concerned—intervention in the Greek civil war, missiles for Cuba, Vietnam? When national security at the highest level is at stake and military decisions must be made quickly, economic factors, though not forgotten, take a back seat. When the concern is crisis management—whether or not to bomb North Vietnam or to send troops to Iran—business executives are not consulted. Their role is limited to considering long-term investment policies. In recent years, though the business of government may to a large degree be the nurturing of economic corporate growth, the influence of the individual corporations on policy seems to be on the wane. The economic influence remains, along with the general pressure upon government to maintain a healthy economic climate, but the power of decision-making rests more and more with the state and is specifically wielded by a small clique of advisers, most of whom, it must be admitted, have been recruited from the leading corporate enterprises. These cliques, which Franklin D. Roosevelt first called his Brain Trust, are today more commonly referred to as the National Security Managers.

The National Security Managers

The French Premier Georges Clemenceau observed, "Modern war is too serious a business to be entrusted to soldiers." The direct responsibility seems to be with men who are considered to be great and thoughtful statesmen advised by the brightest brains available. Their decisions are not made from a welling-over of aggression. They are decisions made far from any fighting, with no more emotion, for the most part, than one invests in choosing between television shows. They certainly are not expressions of the will of the American people or the Russian people, nor are they made by corporate executives. Since World War II they have emanated from the President and his group of chosen advisers.

Until June 19, 1940, national security was primarily a congressional prerogative. On that date President Roosevelt appointed Henry L. Stimson Secretary of War. Stimson's recruits became the architects of the national security planning during World War II and after. For the most part they were bankers and lawyers, whose habits of mind tended to regard the United States as a business client and all other countries as natural competitors. As a group, such men lacked the education and outlook to understand people whose circumstances fell short of their own Ivy League background, a definite limitation in the implementation of foreign relations where there are over 3 billion such people.

President Roosevelt had his "troubleshooter," Harry Hopkins, to help him circumvent a bumbling Congress. As he added more advisers, the role of Congress diminished. Following this trend, President Kennedy not only tried to bypass Congress but established his own "streamlined bureaucracies" to supplement the State Department, which he described as a "bowl of jelly." These security advisers were hand-picked men upon whom the President was obliged to depend heavily in the decision-making process, and to a large extent President

Kennedy's biggest contribution to future policies was made at the time he recruited his advisers. They were bright young men for the most part, men dedicated to hard work and personal success, who, if they were to last as security advisers, mirrored the President's viewpoints and were unwavering in their loyalties to the man they served. The Presidency of the United States is an awesome office, and those who serve it by appointment are quick to realize that their survival is a function not so much of informing, let alone correcting, but of pleasing the President—pleasing, agreeing with him, and providing supportive arguments, making what has been referred to as "the right noises." In addition to supporting the President, the national security adviser, with the United States as ultimate client, sees his primary task as enhancing the national power and influence in the world. Objectivity is rarely his first concern, and objectivity is, of course, an important quality for anyone seeking nonviolent solutions for national security problems, for it helps in seeing the adversary's viewpoint; such uncommon objectivity can lead to charges of supporting the enemy.

Not only does a security adviser need to be partisan where his nation and President are concerned, he must give absolute support to the bureaucratic organization to which he belongs, for his continued employment depends upon its remaining a vital contributor to the government. This lower-level partisanship maintains an atmosphere of struggle and bargaining between the various agencies with overlapping functions. Classic is the perpetual contest among the military services for arms appropriations, resulting in redundant weapons systems. Unidentified but ominous objects in the Soviet Union are identified as new aircraft by the U. S. Air Force's intelligence officers, as tanks by Army observers.

The cold war has not been a time that favored conciliation among the elite of national security advisers. "Toughness" is the quality that is preferred. It almost always pays off. General William Westmoreland, whose advice undoubtedly did much to escalate the disaster in Vietnam, might have been relieved had he considered conciliation or withdrawal. As it was, he won the appointment of Army Chief of Staff.

Probably the strongest incentive to become a security adviser is the desire to wield power. One such adviser confessed to a psychoanalyst that the persistent dream of his childhood was to rule the world. Wars may be unwanted, but it is not surprising that men of such disposition frequently interpret the often inadequate facts in such a way as to conclude that war is unavoidable. Not only does the nature of the task appeal to power-hungry, narrowly patriotic men; it may well attract those of a malignant turn of mind, dutiful bureaucrats on the surface, like Hitler's commander of the SS, Heinrich Himmler, whose energies so willingly gravitated to the service of war and mass murder. There were fortunately none of his ilk evident in the cliques of advisers who served Presidents Kennedy and Johnson, and yet such men, with their sharp intellects and perceptions, promoted and perpetuated a shameful and misguided war for over a decade.

What has been described as the security advisers' "finest hour" was the Cuban missile crisis, when they gambled the fate of civilization and came up winners. More than money, more than fame, they had the exhilarating sense of playing for high stakes. As several have since admitted in their memoirs, they loved the excitement. As is the usual case with bureaucratic homicide, they had the thrill of planning the killing without the ugly burden of physically carrying it out. At the same time the managers of national security require living enemies, for without a threat their task becomes meaningless. In connection with ferreting out potential enemies, Vietnam came to the fore. The French were pulling out of their former colony. World communism, it was said, would fill the vacuum. Ignored was the fact that the Vietnamese had been fighting foreign intruders for hundreds of years; ignored was a CIA report indicating that the communization of Vietnam would not act as a falling domino, toppling one Southeast Asian government after another; ignored was a 1962 report from Michael Forrestal, a White House assistant and close friend of President Kennedy's, stating that most of the recruits serving against the official South Vietnamese government were of local origin and not infiltrators from the North, as was being publicly claimed. Early in the Kennedy administration, when the United States response to the unrest in South Vietnam was being weighed, the President sent General Maxwell Taylor to Saigon for a recommendation. One wonders about the result if he had sent instead a Harvard sociologist. General Taylor, faithful to military solutions, returned with the inevitable recommendation. Kennedy could hardly have been surprised. Armed intervention by the United States subsequently increased.

After Kennedy's untimely death, Lyndon Johnson moved into the White House. Johnson had a simple approach to dealing with foreigners, which he elaborated in a story to reporters before becoming President. It concerned Mexican migrants who would become squatters on the front lawn if you let them. The next day they'd plant their barefoot 130-pound bodies on the porch, and the day after, take over the whole house. But if you let them know right off you weren't going to put up with it, you and the Mexicans would get on just fine.

Vietnamese were barefoot, too, and didn't weigh a bit more than Mexicans, and even if it was their own lawn he was talking about, Johnson tried to apply the same formula. He was a strong and intimidating man. His advisers fell readily into line. They told him he was doing the right thing. It took years for the American public to conclude otherwise, whereupon Johnson chose not to run again for office. Richard Nixon, pledged to a policy of peace, succeeded him, but even Nixon had a flirtation with victory. He ordered the sudden invasion of

Cambodia. Why did he feel justified in doing so? Very largely because his security advisers had worked out such a plan, and such contingency plans are based upon the presumption of success, never defeat. They amount to a psychological certification of victory.

In the end, of course, under growing public pressure and disillusionment among the security advisers themselves, the United States withdrew from Vietnam. The Army had fired off an average of one ton of copper per man per year in Vietnam to preserve its world image, which presumably might help in the future acquisition of scarce materials, such as copper, at bargain prices. To the extent that the war was economically motivated, would it not have been cheaper to pay premium prices for copper? The question is too painfully rational and benefited by hindsight. War is rarely a rational business, and with Vietnam the real question was, why did it take public reaction against the war so long to develop?

The Public

The public is unfortunately very vulnerable to manipulation on issues of national security. For the most part it does not even need manipulation, because it isn't very much interested. As far as pressure groups are concerned, be they farmers, factory workers, or white-collar employees, their political interests are domestic and specifically concerned with getting a fair slice of the economic pie. Big international issues less and less concern the Congress; even less do they involve the electorate in party campaigns.

One problem is secrecy. Secrecy has long been considered the privilege of kings. It abides at the heart of power itself. To lie secretly in wait is the very essence of the predatory act, and the presumption remains that the world is a deadly place and the President must be able to act quickly and secretly, a presumption seemingly ennobled by the instantaneous nature of thermonuclear war. Once the right of secrecy in high places is conceded, it becomes a most effective device for shaping public opinion, for it places the security managers in the impregnable position of being able to say, "But you wouldn't say that if you knew what we know." This is intimidating, and usually the public acknowledges its own ignorance, although in actual fact the intelligence gap between the managers and the public exists less in regard to the world situation than to the clandestine and guarded actions of the security managers themselves. The public has access to the news as reported by other nations, and the press in the United States is as free from government censorship as anywhere else, though it often comes under pressure to support the foreign policy of the government. More subtly, a reporter who is indiscreet may be deprived of "access" to certain officials. A reporter may be encouraged to magnify or play down a certain event. Another tactic is the official "leak" of information, which, since it seems to come without government sanction, gains an undeserved aura of authenticity. Not uncommonly the military services, before pressuring for increased arms expenditures, will "leak" classified material tending to announce new and awesome Soviet weaponry.

Unlike most animals, human beings are capable of anticipating future dangers. This ability means they can be hoodwinked into imagining danger that has no reality. It is highly inconvenient from the government's point of view for citizens to make private judgments regarding the magnitude of these international dangers, and the citizen who is overly insistent may well run afoul of Selective Service laws, not to mention those concerned with treason. To avoid such unpleasantness, it is the business of the managers of national security to "educate" the public. The average citizen can be counted on to cooperate with a degree of apathy. In countries without our democratic tradition, foreign policy has always been the business of the governmental elite, with the citizens expected to offer up money and sons when the band begins to play. In the United States, however, the citizen has a "right to know," but in the mind of the security manager what the citizen knows should be skillfully prepared so that a reluctant public will not impede diplomatic flexibility. More positively, the Joint Chiefs of Staff look for a unified "national will" at the crux of national power. To turn normal apathy into this state of arousal, an aura of crisis is required. To create this mood without binding the government's diplomatic hands, the security managers must be very tactful in their artistry. When asked by an interviewer whether the citizenry had a "right to know" about foreign policy-making, General Maxwell Taylor replied very candidly, "A citizen should know those things he needs to be a good citizen and to discharge his functions." Presumably, discharging his functions includes going to war enthusiastically if the President so decrees. To avoid war, the crisis need only be downplayed and the public will remain uninterested. When war seems appropriate, the managers get busy "preparing public opinion" for possible conflict. The "vital interests" of the United States are seen to be threatened; perhaps the "Free World" is at stake.

War-minded leaders have long been skillful at winning public support with the right words. United States participation in World War II, which may have been inevitable, was nonetheless exhaustively prepared by President Roosevelt, so that Clare Boothe Luce might say with unkind accuracy, "He lied us into war because he did not have the courage to lead us." Probably it had nothing to do with courage, only an intuitive sense of how best to ready a reluctant public for war.

At this point, public manipulation is more a science than an art form. The real reasons for fighting a war may be too unsavory or too complex for public consumption. The primary and most effective public stimulant is fear. Throughout the cold war it was the annual business of the Pentagon to leak topsecret intelligence about innovations in Russian weaponry. The "year of maximum danger" was always at hand. Along

with fear, another emotion to be strummed was that of guilt:
the Christian duty to stand by one's friends and honor international commitments.

   In preparing the national mood for Vietnam, two myths had
to be popularized: first, that the attack on South Vietnam had
come from the North. When enthusiasm flagged for supporting
this poor, peace-loving people, President Johnson took the
guilt ploy so far as to brand war critics as racists who did not
care about the fate of yellow Asiatics. The fear tactic depended
on the "domino" myth that if South Vietnam went Communist, so would one Asian country after another until the United
States stood alone in a hostile world. Righteous rage on the
part of the American public was anticipated as soon as American blood had been shed, and this business of "First Blood"
has been noted as a time-honored ritual of any war. When the
security managers are having a hard time demonstrating that
vital American interests are at stake in a war that is difficult to
locate on the map, continuing blood sacrifice becomes even
more important. The very redemption of those who otherwise
may have died in vain becomes a guilt factor, and those who go
on fighting become themselves a vital interest. Another emotion helpful to a war effort is hatred of "the enemy"—never
"an enemy" or even "our enemy," but "the enemy," as
though the foe were indeed the protagonist of all mankind.
Thus divested of his humanity, he becomes a hostile and evil
force for which compassion is impossible. The mood was
achieved with considerable justice in World War II, but failed
utterly during the Vietnam conflict.

   The most notorious manipulators of public sentiment were
Adolf Hitler and his Minister of Propaganda, Joseph Goebbels.
Propaganda has become a dirty word thanks to these two—
security managers today prefer to "educate." Hitler had no
sense of moral restraint. The only measure, as far as he was
concerned, was success. The goal was world conquest; the
method of preparing the German people was whatever

worked. The rules of the game were simple: emphasize the most basic public fears and stress solutions in keeping with your objectives. In *Mein Kampf* (*My Struggle*) Hitler wrote: "To whom has propaganda to appeal? To the scientific intelligentsia or to the less-educated masses? It has to appeal forever and only to the masses." As Goebbels later elaborated: "The ordinary man hates nothing more than two-sidedness, to be called upon to consider this as well as that. The masses think simply and primitively. They love to generalize complicated situations and from their generalization to draw clear and uncompromising conclusions." As Hitler meant to impart emotions rather than facts, he preferred a susceptible audience, a weary, uncritical evening audience in a close-packed auditorium. He never, if possible, submitted his comments to paper, lest they be subjected to the criticism of rational analysis, but recorded in *Mein Kampf* that ". . . one is able to win people far more by the spoken than by the written word, and . . . every great movement on this globe owes its rise to the great speakers and not to the great writers." Hitler sensed what later research confirmed, that "the mass of people is lazy in itself, that they lazily remain within the course of old habits, and that by themselves they do not like to take up anything written unless it corresponds to what one believes oneself, and furnishes what one hopes for." In addition to beer halls, stadiums, and auditoriums, Hitler's personal voice campaign was aided by radio. One shudders to speculate upon what success he would have achieved by appearing on television.

No significant foreign policy decision has ever been made in response to spontaneous public demand, though a hostile public reaction has a definite impact on national leadership. The public lacks power and organization to transcribe its temper swiftly into political change, but it can make its leaders uncomfortable. Although adverse public opinion, in its effect on policy, may be depressingly slow, a government of thousands cannot determine the behavior of millions year after year. In the long run, stability requires a degree of genuine consent, and for this reason a government must explain itself to obtain the agreement or at least the passive acquiesence of the public. That is why political ideologies are so fervently pressed, for the rulers of any nation fear nothing so much as loss of faith in its political ideals on the part of the public.

In the case of Vietnam, disillusionment became public long before it could be accepted by President Johnson and his sycophantic clique of advisers. The process took years, for the majority of private citizens must sense they are being hurt by foreign policy before they will deny support to the expansionist designs carefully wrapped in a patriotic flag. This self-consciousness came variously, from foreign criticism of the war policy in general, from those who had relatives directly involved, from a business community that began to see the war as bad business, and from an aroused body of young citizens in whom a genuine sense of internationalism seemed to have initiated identification with foreigners as human beings rather than as stereotypes. There was much shame in the Vietnam War, but also much to be proud of. Young Americans loved their country enough to refuse a blank check to its Administration, in the name of patriotism, when the policies of that governing body seemed to contradict the high standards of liberty and freedom for which the nation has stood.

Of course, a sudden thermonuclear war would allow no such public soul-searching. Here the public would remain helpless, at the mercy of its government and its rivals. Nor is there much comfort in assuming that, even with misguided brushfire wars of the Vietnam type, public reaction requires ten years to galvanize itself. All this does not add up to a comfortable prognosis for the average peace-loving human in a society structured for war, but it need not be a death sentence for the race. Vietnam was a defeat, but not such a catastrophe as overtook the empires of the nineteenth century, and it was a warning and a lesson to the American public and the military-industrial-governmental complex that spawned and perpetuated it.

The Lessons of Vietnam

Militarily we learned a great deal in Vietnam. We learned that the Pentagon can become overly involved in the making of international policies. Though the military establishment will continue to have a hand in policy-making, nevertheless it is not apt to be so heavy a hand, nor will its opinions be accepted as uncritically as in the past. In terms of actually conducting such wars, this much has been learned: military force in the Third World does not pay off. Where resistance on the part of a people is so strong that an army is required to suppress them, the price of supporting imperial prerogatives far exceeds the benefit to be gained.

There are, of course, many of a military bent who would still maintain that the only error in Vietnam was the tragic underestimating of the enemy strength. If the sole objective was crushing those Orientals who opposed us, this is undeniable, but over the long course of the cold war a good case can be made that an overestimating of the enemy's strength may be a greater danger. The accepted Pentagon policy has been so-called worst-case planning: that is, assume the worst and be able to match it. Cheap insurance, perhaps, but such planning leads to endless back-and-forth escalation of military spending. As long as we arm ourselves on the basis of a succession of imaginary terrors on the part of a potential opponent, he will do so as well, ad infinitum, while the more proper test for the sufficiency of our retaliatory might is not our worst judgment of its effectiveness but the opponent's assessment of the damage it would endure in an atomic confrontation.

The business community learned a lot from Vietnam, which went against the conventional wisdom that business profits when the government militarily supports economic imperialism.

In theory, of course, the business community could easily be cured of its link to the military. All private profit could be taken out of war preparations. Imagine a law that said that when war was waged and young men and possibly women were drafted, industry would be treated as public property for the duration, a kind of wartime socialism, with salaries comparable to a military pay scale. After all, if human lives could be drafted into national service, why not property?

Most important, of course, in curbing a drift to warlike foreign policies is to place some restraints upon the national security managers, so that they may not again inflict their imperialist imaginings on the American public. Congress has very largely abdicated its constitutional rights in this regard. It should reestablish them. The planners must be held accountable for their policy-making. It is too easy to attribute results to "impersonal forces" beyond human control. The system should be reevaluated so that, all things being equal, the peacemaker, not the war-maker, is rewarded. A subpoena to the Secretary of Defense, not to mention a batch of subpoenas to his security advisers, compelling testimony on one of his clandestine wars, would go far to rectify the balance of constitutional powers.

If the United States is not to become a military society, its civilian representatives must retain the final rights to deciding issues of peace and war. The Vietnam War was certainly a setback for the promilitary clique, but this does not mean that the supporters of real peace are in the ascendancy. If our official policy is more noninterventionist than before, it remains easy to shout "No More Vietnams" while insisting on ever higher "defense" budgets. If the consensus now is that Vietnam was a mistake, it must be remembered that it was not an accident. Wars never are, and the best hope is that such mistakes will become less common. There are hopeful modifications in attitude. Even some union officials are beginning to note the impact of war upon inflation, the decline of buying power, and the breakdown of social services. There is deep aversion to another such military imbroglio, but it must be recalled that the Korean War elicited a like, if less adamant, response. Are we perhaps moving toward a foreign policy of peace? Defenders of the old imperial ways have already branded this emerging attitude as the "new isolationism," and that in itself is a favorable sign. Even if it is impossible to put an end to the war power, mankind's values regarding that power may be changed as part of a growing internationalism, with the wisdom to realize that before the world can be made truly safe for Russian communism or American capitalism it must be made safe for all humanity.

FOUR

Swords or Plowshares

*. . . and they shall beat their swords into plowshares,
and their spears into pruning hooks; nations shall not
lift up sword against nation, neither shall they learn
war any more.*

Isaiah 2:4

The Dangers

They say that Groucho Marx once asked, "What has posterity
ever done for me?" Nothing, perhaps, beyond raising the prospect of a kind of vicarious immortality, that "better world" to
which we vaguely strive in moments of idealism. Value posterity or not, the human race today seems bent on destroying
the inheritance of the unborn. Is this foolish pessimism? Man
has overcome every obstacle in his path before—surely he will
overcome those of his own making? And is this not overopti-
mistic? One zoologist has speculated that our stubborn optimism has been bred into us during the process of evo-

161

lution, creating an inherent arrogance that cannot confront the gravity of today's global situation, a situation resulting from an era of anarchy, want, and suffering. World wars tormented the first half of this century; their renewal could finish the second; and short of such open conflict we can expect unprecedented convulsive change brought about by external events, not by choice. The approaching historical crisis that by some is seen as a major turning point cannot be avoided; it can only be mitigated by concerted effort worldwide. Yet all nations remain preoccupied with their limited problems and needs on a very short-term basis, while the four horsemen of the Apocalypse, their names updated but deadly still, thunder toward us: Population Explosion; Failure of Resources; Environmental Degradation; Thermonuclear Abuse.

Consider the human population first, perhaps 7 million at the birth of agriculture, 300 million when Christ was crucified, three times that number when the American colonies fought for independence. The numbers redoubled by 1900, more than redoubled by 1975, when 4 billion humans laid claim to their birth rights. At present world population is doubling every thirty-six years, and already every expert in the field would say without hesitation that for the optimum fulfillment of life it has long since exceeded acceptable limits.

Communist China, with its authoritarian system, has had a limited success in controlling its birth rate. It may be a sad fact of the future that only such authoritarian governments, able to demand obedience, will be able to successfully cope with the problem. The rest of the underdeveloped world, lacking the ideological intensity and regimented discipline, has had little success at population control. When a United Nations group met at Bucharest in 1974 to discuss world population problems, nothing was achieved; in fact, many southern "have-not" nations regard birth control as a device fostered by rich white northern nations to keep down the swarms of the poor and nonwhite. "May you have seventeen sons and sixteen daughters" is the Indonesian wedding toast, and one not spoken in jest, in a land already smothering in its own humanity.

Overcrowding not only lowers the quality of life for any species, it is the breeding ground of hostility and has been a time-honored cause of war, with sparsely settled areas acting like the suction of a vacuum upon overpopulated ones. The philosopher Thomas Hobbes, who set the stage for Charles Darwin, held that overpopulation was the primary cause of war and that it would put an end to future wars by putting an end to the world.

Hand in hand with overpopulation comes the exhaustion of resources, the most basic of which is food. The American shopper complains about the soaring price of beef. In other countries, people starve for want of grain. Charles Darwin in his theory of the origin of species hypothesized that creatures multiply faster than their food supply, thus causing a perpetual competition for the means of survival. As the planet becomes increasingly overcrowded, and the questions of living space and nutrition more vital, the likelihood of conflict intensifies.

A few years ago the discovery of "miracle" strains of high-yield cereals was proclaimed as the splendid solution to human starvation, but in practice these grains have not found their way into the shrunken bellies of the poor; they have gone to fatten the livestock of the rich. About a third of the world's cereal produce, in fact, feeds northern livestock, and, when the United States has a grain surplus, it goes not to Indian peasants but to Soviet cattle. After all, a modern farmer works for profit. Nebraska farmers, at least until the Russian invasion of Afghanistan, grew grain for the highest bidder's cattle. For the moment we struggle along. Conveniently, those suffering from malnutrition have little vitality left over for loud protest, and death by starvation is a singularly quiet process. But just suppose the polar ice caps were to expand, and temperatures decline a few degrees. It happened 90,000 years ago; it will again. Then the grain crops in Canada, the northern United States, the Soviet Union, China, Australia, and Argentina would vanish, all within less than a century.

This may sound improbable, but an average drop of 1 degree Celsius shortens the growing season of Russian crops by two weeks, enough to cause 27 percent crop damage. Suppose a few cold years, and another phenomenon known as *albedo* must be considered. Albedo is the reflection of sunlight from the earth's surface. The more sunlight the earth reflects—and there is nothing like ice and snow to do the job—the cooler it gets. Once the phenomenon is set in motion by two or three cold winters, it is self-serving: more ice to reflect—cooler air to make more ice. Within a few years the impact on the food supply could be disastrous.

The United States and its industrialized contemporaries are just now more concerned with diminishing petroleum supplies. Armies can't function without it, summer holidays are spoiled without gasoline, food can't be delivered without fuel for trucks. The historian Lynn White, Jr., has blamed Christianity for much of today's problem; it is a criticism applicable to any man-centered religion. Many older beliefs, such as those still nurtured by American Indians, retain a kinship with and respect for nature, but when man is elevated to a position of dominion over nature, deliberate exploitation of the environment follows naturally.

In recklessly using the resources of this earth, Western man has not only squandered them but initiated a dangerous ecological backlash with his wastes. The nature of human economy is self-consuming. Unlike any species before us, we have unbalanced nature and seem determined to destroy our own environment. The consumption of energy, primarily derived from fossil fuels, has increased threefold since World War II. At such a rate, petroleum and natural gas will be exhausted in fifty years. Nuclear power with its poisonous wastes and explosive hazards is clearly no long-term answer. Many other vital raw materials are in diminishing supply. Thus far the capitalist economies have been affected only with inflationary costs, unemployment, and recession. Yet material growth remains an objective not only of the capitalist countries but of China and the Soviet Union. All their official ideologies deny this limitation of materials. The finite shortage of earthly resources must intensify conflict, particularly between the "have" nations of the north and the "have-nots" of the south. Eventually money may not serve to buy what a nation needs. Quite possibly, wars will be justified on this basis if equitable international means of distribution have not been established. The industrial response to any threat to their supplies may well be furious. There has already been the Suez war of 1956 when Egyptian seizure of the Canal was taken as a threat to sever "Britain's jugular."

In 1975 the average American represented over $7,000 in gross national product. The average Indian represented only $150, yet was better off than the citizens of fifteen other countries. The gap widens. Populations in industrialized areas are almost stable. In poor, underdeveloped parts of the globe people multiply, their poverty becoming additionally unbearable when they can daily compare it with the relative opulence of others. Will they tranquilly leave a class of favored nations indefinitely in exclusive possession of the good life? Even if the answer is yes, how long can the rich north maintain its own standard of living? Since World War II the United States has moved from a position of near self-sufficiency to one of increasing dependency on foreign sources of supply. This is true throughout most of the industrialized world.

At the moment, the average northerner in his lifetime uses fifty times more of the world's diminishing resources than an Indian peasant. Capitalism with its drive and urgency, its quotas and hard sell, its nuclear reactors, smokestacks, missiles, and deteriorating ecology, remains dedicated to expanding output. With the Third World starving around us, the ground being cemented over beneath our feet, and thermonuclear war a sword of Damocles above us, the wealthy nations of the world remain obsessed with secondary problems. Billions go for armaments and gas-guzzling passenger cars. A few millions for cancer research, a ghastly disease on the upswing in industrial society, in large part thanks to the absorption of pollutants of our own creation, but not a cent for bilharzia. Whoever heard of bilharzia? It is a wasting parasitic disease that attacks over 200 million of the Third World's poor. The industrial nations are not to blame. They didn't create the disease, nor do they intend the economic stagnation of the south, though they run a system that leads to that result. Investments in agriculture have benefitted big farmers rather than small peasants. Major public works such as bridges and paved roads provide brief labor, with very little effect upon the poorest who must walk regardless, while serving primarily to speed the military vehicles of the army clique that is in power.

In the past it has been said that it is the privilege of the great to observe disaster from a terrace. No more. World environment, diminishing supplies of energy and resources, threaten the viability of all industrial systems. Given the customary human behavior, the ties of national identity are sure to exert growing pressures, mobilizing national loyalties while inhibiting the international sharing of wealth and burdens. Even amid abundance, capitalist societies have never been overly successful in creating an atmosphere of social harmony. The privileged will not easily accept the shrinking of their bounty. Democratic institutions within the structure of capitalist society will probably lack the capacity to cope with the polarizing of strife between have and have-nots. Government will probably resort to increasingly authoritarian means. If the economic pressures are bound to increase within the various industrial societies, what hope is there to reconcile their strivings with the needs of the Third World nations? After all, who has the slightest concern for the black, brown, and yellow masses? They are strange and distant people, not our responsibility unless we regard the world as a global village with the fate of one the fate of all. If this uncommon idea of a shared humanity does not acquire motivating strength—and soon—we may all be lost. Nor is this intended to ascribe any natural wisdom to the Third World. Far from it. In the main they regard the ecology outcry on the part of industrialized nations as a plot to keep them a sort of backward tourist paradise and game park. When given the chance, they despoil the environment as energetically as the rest of us. So our present course is toward a gradual impoverishment of life. The alternatives are a change in attitude or war.

Future Wars

Unprecedented pressures that have made for wars in the past exist in the world today. Civil wars and limited wars involving emergent nations are common and taken for granted. Unlimited wars are dreaded. As the near-certainty of a thermonuclear clash between the Soviet Union and the United States seems to diminish, the specter of another, more fundamental confrontation begins to form, the rich white industrial northern nations versus the poor black or brown rural south. The lines are clearly drawn: the old imperialist powers lined up against their recent vassals, a nearly classic Marxian struggle with racial overtones. (In South Africa, the industrialized Japanese are regarded as white.)

At the moment the technology for such a war is not sufficiently distributed, but the process is taking place, and, as has already been noted, the very impersonal magnitude of these weapons is a psychological factor to be reckoned with. Morality has made progress over the centuries. We appear to be more sensitive to human suffering than were our ancestors. Few politicians applaud, even privately, the statements of nineteenth-century militarists who saluted war as "the health of the state," but technology has more than wiped out morality's refinement by making mass killing possible without fury, without effort, and with very little sense of guilt. This technology has left us with only fear and suspicion, inducing most nations to spend the larger part of their substance on arsenals, thereby depriving their citizens of much needed sanitation, shelter, food, and clothing, not to mention such refinements as medical care, parks, libraries, and schools.

If there is some effort to limit the spread of nuclear weapons, such is not the case with conventional weapons, an export trade in which the United States ranks first. The impoverished south spends infinitely more on these arms than on education, health, and birth control. It is not for want of trying that the impoverished nations still lack the capacity for inflicting Armageddon on the world, and it will not be long until that most dangerous of potentials has proliferated worldwide. From proliferation the obvious path leads on to the unthinkable, thermonuclear war. All the plagues visited by God upon the Egyptians would be as nothing in comparison. Humanity has in this way supplanted God and taken into its own hands the ultimate tools of divine judgment. Many American Indians believe that the 1990s will encompass the apocalypse. The Mayans of Central America are more specific: the world will be destroyed on December 24, 2011. The Hindus call this the age of Kali-Yuga, the time of darkness, when the god Shiva lifts on high the purifying fire. One may dismiss them as myths, of course, and yet they do give the imagination pause.

There are pessimists who say fine, let the war come: only by such a calamity would the survivors learn their lesson and make those sweeping changes necessary to put an end to war. Yet a small disquieting voice asks: Have we not had such traumatic shocks before? The trenches of World War I, Auschwitz, and Hiroshima all in their time were taken as starting points for a moral recoil from future wars, and yet since 1945 we have learned to live quite complacently with the bomb.

Some experts feel that yes, we may seem complacent, but deep down the apocalyptic fear is so great, and the fruitlessness of such a war so obvious, that it will never be fought. Let us hope so, but even if mankind contrives to evade a widespread nuclear war, there is no reason to expect it to curtail more limited violence within the foreseeable future. This can take a variety of forms: all-out wars conducted by classic armies as in the past; limited wars; civil disturbances, particularly acts of terrorism. All-out wars on the part of nuclear powers, exempting that weapon only, seem unlikely. True, poison gas was not used on the battlefield in World War II, but it was never a decisive weapon, and it seems likely that nuclear powers, once backed to the wall, would have final resort to their most powerful weapons. The psychology of this situation has not been tested, and it has been the policy of the United States not to renounce atomic weapons. As Eisenhower's Secretary of Defense Charles E. Wilson once said, "We can't afford to fight limited wars. We can only afford to fight a big one, and if there is one, that is the kind it will be." This theory is based primarily on the larger Soviet population and the USSR's capacity to field more men. In practice, however, the United States has been involved only in limited wars, and there are those who feel that if we mean to survive they are the only sort of war we can afford to fight. In a Department of the Army pamphlet, *Bibliography on Limited War* (February 1958), Chief of Staff General Maxwell D. Taylor summed up the case for limited war: "In these days of dramatic satellite launchings and missile flights, public attention is to a large degree focused on the dangers of a possible general thermonuclear war. This concern is understandable, but it may cause us to overlook the equally serious threat of limited wars initiated by an aggressor under the protective cover of mutual nuclear deterrence. Limited aggression, if not arrested, could lead to the possible loss of much of the Free World and, if not quickly suppressed, might spread into the general conflagration, which we hope to avoid. I consider, therefore, that our readiness to fight and win promptly any local conflict is of the utmost importance, not only to discourage potential enemies from limited military adventures, but as one of the major deterrents to general atomic war itself."

So far the restraint, thanks to good sense and restricted availability of the bomb, has held good. The passage of time, however, acts as a statistical factor mitigating against the probability that this restriction will last forever. The prospect of retaliation in kind would give any nation pause, but what about that new suicidal element, the international terrorist? There is a morbid mentality to whom a nuclear bomb might seem a heaven-sent gift.

Supposing, as some optimists do, that thermonuclear weapons have rendered the old form of extreme international violence obsolete, the human race is still left with its loyalties and hatreds, its fringe group of passionate killers who seek to express their political discontents in the most conspicuous and violent fashion available. These are the international terrorists, and in late 1971 they conducted an ominous meeting in Florence, Italy. Representatives came from sixteen revolutionary movements in the hope of extending their global activities. Present were members of the time-honored Irish Republican Army, who subsequently trained and armed Basque separatists who murdered Spanish Prime Minister Admiral Luis Carrero Blanco. The ERP from Argentina was present, seeking arms from German contacts. There were Tupamaros from South America, named for the last great Inca chief Tupac Amaru, who brought death to his Spanish conquerors, and Frelimos from Portuguese Africa intent on creating a rebel Pan-African movement, all in agreement on one common purpose: the overthrow of world order by force and violence. The savage international implications of this meeting became clear on May 30, 1972, in Israel's Lod Airport where a happy crowd of religious tourists from Puerto Rico were waiting to claim their luggage. Three short, tidy young Oriental men waited with them until, almost by magic, they produced Czech-made submachine guns which they began firing at random into the close-packed crowd. Hand grenades followed, and before two of the assassins lay dead—one from his own grenade which went off when he slipped on the blood of his victims—twenty-seven tourists also were dead and seventy-five were injured. To what purpose? Answers came from the one surviving killer who was captured when his ammunition ran out. "Slaughter and destruction are inevitable. I warn the entire world. The Red Army will slay anyone who is on the side of the bourgeois. Revolutionary warfare must be worldwide. Our struggle will become more severe than warfare between nations." So spoke Kozo Akomoto, who had come around the world to kill Puerto Ricans in an Israeli airport with Czechoslovakian weapons. Truly, international terrorism had come of age. The Red Army of which he spoke was not the vast legions of Soviet Russia but a handpicked clique of Japanese men and women dignifying their frenzied intent under the title "United Red Army." What makes this group so deadly (and there are many of a like mentality) is their willingness, even eagerness, to die in behalf of their objectives. Nuclear terrorism remains a brooding and ominous possibility for the future. And what about the employment of terrorists by the have-not nations as a threat, if not an actuality, in wars for the redistribution of wealth? At the present rate, impoverished nations may have no other course.

Change Without War?

If the world is experiencing ever stronger pressures toward

war, movement toward a new peaceful world format is just as evident. Sooner or later, all mankind on this shrinking globe must, if we are to survive, participate in a single world culture. In terms of ecology-resources-travel-survival, the world's people are closer together than the thirteen American colonies were in 1775. As the French writer Albert Camus said, "No economic problem, however minor it appears, can be solved outside the comity of nations." Argentine wheat is eaten in Europe, Siberian machine tools are made in Detroit. Today, tragedy is collective. So is security. With the report of a new type of virus in the Soviet Union, citizens in New York dutifully line up to take flu shots developed in Switzerland. They get back into their Japanese cars, eat at a French restaurant, see an Italian movie, return home to drink South American coffee before an English TV show, shower and dry off with towels made in the Republic of China, put on pajamas made in Korea, and finally dream about a photographic safari in East Africa. Instantaneous worldwide communication, transportation at comparable speed, weather control, exploitation of the common oceans and outer space, all press toward globalism, like it or not. And globalism is not limited to the opulent. Hardly anyone on earth can live unaware of technology. As soon as the isolated peasant sees a transistor radio, he wants it, and as soon as he has it, the old ways that have satisfied him for centuries are forever diminished. Now nothing exists in isolation, not individuals or states. All have global extensions, implications, and consequences. It is impossible to regard global cooperation as merely a crackpot ideal of ivory-towered intellectuals. It is a first rule for survival.

With world politics and technology pushing all nations, including the United States and the Soviet Union, to work via international institutions, still we exist in a period of intensified nationalism that makes cooperation in the short run difficult. Considering the number of sovereign states brought into

being since World War II, many of them torn by internal conflicts, it is surprising that so little, rather than so much, violence has accompanied the vast displacements of loyalty
groups. Deeply entrenched are the forces of cultural particu-
larism, and regardless of the impact of globalism, world peace
will never be achieved through the simplistic doctrine of "better understanding among people." It has been hypothesized
that war between Germany and France is no longer imaginable
because the two peoples have come to know each other so
well. The theory is that they no longer can be aroused by abstract images of "the enemy." Undoubtedly this is true to an
extent for all people, at least in terms of mutual understanding
of superficial customs and constitutions, but the hypothesis
that it will prevent war by impeding governments in their creation of the devil image of rival peoples flies against the fact.
Physical nearness, even over long periods of time, has not prevented the cruelest forms of violence. Civil wars are characteristically more savagely fought than international wars. Mutual
intimacy is as likely to foster hatred as it is to dispel it. Contact
between expanding and competitive groups is often a starting
point for violence. Situations demanding intergroup cooperation, particularly when survival is at stake, are what dispel antagonism.

Today that sort of attitude of worldwide cooperation is badly
needed. The earth is one boat, and we are all in it. The march
of civilization has been steadily toward the formation of larger
social units. Under conditions prevailing in the eighteenth century, with continents separated at best by long and desperate
sea voyages, the widest feasible area for sovereignty was the
nation. Today, as has already been pointed out, the idea of the
nation-state is obsolete. It can no longer seriously protect its
citizens against foreign aggression and the disasters that war
brings. Today's global situation has done more than bankrupt
the idea of the nation-state. It has superseded our explanations

of the world and the simple faiths of the past. A vacuum exists between traditions of a vanishing past and fresh knowledge of the universe. New, more realistic philosophies concerning the world and our role in it are necessary if humanity is to survive. The question is, can we make these necessary adjustments in thought and deed while there is still time?

One geneticist theorized that animal species can evolve and alter significant intellectual and emotional traits, and all within no more than ten generations—a very promising prognosis for short-lived fruit flies, but in the case of human beings the same changes would take, theoretically, some three hundred years, far too long to postpone the threats that gallop toward us. Fortunately humanity has the faculties of reasoning and anticipation, which the fruit fly lacks. These capacities may enable both developed and underdeveloped to come to grips with the global situation. The developed nations, whether professing socialism or capitalism, share a dangerous ethic, that of steady industrial growth. More, bigger, and better—to fall short is to fail, to counsel cutting back is near-heresy. Yet our present full-throttle policies of exploitation are on a collision course with the world's finite limits.

The biggest single step is to change capitalistic gears from full ahead to neutral. In the first instance, the socialistic nations may have an easier time adjusting to a stationary economy, as their economies are substantially in governmental hands. But in the long run industrial societies, whether Socialist, Communist, or capitalist, will face the same problem, that of curtailing the mode of massive industrial production that is the crowning achievement of all these systems.

Though expansion has been considered inherent in past capitalism, stationary capitalism is not thereby inconceivable, but it will require a government ready to promote a very much modified hierarchy of values and willing to assume an unpopular burden of austerity if national dependence on foreign re-

sources is to be reduced. The postindustrial society of tomorrow must be as distinct from today's industrial world as the
latter is from the agricultural community of the past. Worldwide corporations can no longer milk dependent countries as
before. They must be reconciled to lower profits or, as is the
trend, pass added costs on to the consumer.

The processes of resource consumption may no longer be
applauded as social triumphs, but at best as unavoidable evils
to be reduced to a minimal portion of economic life. This implies, if mankind is to adjust, an across-the-board reassess-
ment of the means of production, which eventually promises
the end of great industrial corporations, huge factories, and
growing urban centers.

If the industrial nations must reappraise their goals, the underdeveloped nations have been given no choice. The only
question is whether their new value systems are appropriate to
the world situation. At the end of World War II, the world
seemed polarized around the Soviet Union and the United
States. A great many new nations were created at this time,
most of them former colonies. There was of course competition, East and West, for their succeeding loyalties, but for the
most part the heady air of independence was not something
they wished to forsake, and as the situation settled, it became
evident that this new group of states would remain politically
aloof as the "Third World." The stalemate between the superpowers was an aid to the position of these nations, as it offered
territorial security between the two as well as economic benefits as a result of the heavy-handed competition between the
United States and the Soviets for their loyalties. But if the
"emergent nations" have been granted their independence,
they have found themselves hopelessly locked into a pattern of
emulation. Like it or not, the inevitable drift is toward Westernization, and the usual result of upheavals in these countries,
however loud and furious their protestations against their

old Western masters, is another step in the same direction, toward the "good life," the material life as described by Western capitalism, which has become a world model for all. Even the Soviet Union, while renouncing capitalistic means, testifies to its dogged pursuit of the same goal with blatant shouts about overtaking and surpassing. Clearly, in so doing, it has accepted the same yardstick by which it measures a very similar definition of progress.

A most impressive and undisguised emulation has been achieved by Japan. Closed to the West until the mid-nineteenth century, Japan constantly rejected Westernization, most violently in World War II, a disaster from which it has emerged a shining example of placid, hardworking capitalism. Few traditional cultures have made the transition with such evident ease. The Western model inflicts a life-style too demanding and complicated for the simpler traditions with which many have lived so long. In most cases these societies have split open, with the privileged and educated taking hold of Western cosmopolitanism and the peasants left poor and without direction amid their evaporating traditions, outsiders in the so-called global city. From this great crowd of outsiders, unless the situation is handled with tactful international cooperation, can be expected outbursts of terrible violence, since their political awakening, as translated and simplified from their Western models, inevitably results in distortion, misunderstanding, and an inability to cope. This in turn leads inevitably to violence, and violence to anarchism or the ascendency of military cliques. The prospects of the Third World nations are not encouraging. With overpopulation and the diminution of vital materials, they can scarcely help falling further behind economically and failing to realize their dreams, dreams that even among the most successful of Western nations are beginning to turn nightmarish. Given the unhappy and unfulfillable aspirations of the underdeveloped world and the painful need of the industrial nations to modify their own cherished values, the extent to which the idea of one world has developed in recent years is surprising.

One World

In this dawning era of world politics, the gap between universalism and nationalism has begun to close. While escalating the war in Vietnam on the one hand, President Lyndon Johnson could blandly declare in his 1965 State of the Union message: "Our own freedom or growth have never been the final goal of the American dream. We were never meant to be an oasis of liberty and abundance in a worldwide desert of disappointed dreams. Our nation was created to help strike away the chains of ignorance and misery and tyranny where they keep man less than God means him to be. . . . What is at stake is the cause of freedom, and in that cause America will never be found wanting."

Two years later, at the anniversary of the Bolshevik revolution, President Leonid Brezhnev of the Soviet Union sounded this similar note: "The homeland country of October, the land of victorious socialism was, is, and will continue to be the hope and mainstay of all the oppressed, of all who are fighting for peace, freedom, and the happiness of peoples."

To a degree, one world exists already. It is loosely held together by a worldwide state system forming power relationships with a common set of standards according to which the various states are ranked. Most underdeveloped states, finding it difficult enough to achieve the goals appropriate to their former cultural seclusion, are swamped by comparisons in this new world setting. Least troubled, of course, is the United States, since our traditional mode of life and aspirations have long been the model for industrial nations as well as the emerging world community. At the bottom of the heap, tribes, clans, and the like have lost out entirely. Kings and queens fare little better. Even Communist countries must nominally bow to the Western democratic model. What we may think of as a strict Communist totalitarian state, East Germany, calls itself the German Democratic Republic and makes an important, if dubiously meaningful, ritual of election day. Good or bad, adults around the world expect to be heard by their governments.

Why should these emerging nations surrender so readily to the ways of aliens they often profess to abhor? Respect, for one thing, in its least attractive form: that is, respect for the armed might that forced them into the colonial posture. In such circumstances it is natural to adopt whatever seems to make their opponent superior. In the first instance this means modern weapons and the Western approach to fighting.

Let us hope that the industrialized West, having bestowed its least worthy characteristics, can lead the way to one peaceful world. There is no going back. There are no historical parallels for guidance. The age of isolation, of migrant hordes, is over. Future conflicts, violent or otherwise, will be contested on a crowded stage before an audience of all humanity. Every successful civilization thus far has been an ongoing step toward cooperation in larger and larger social units. The next meaningful step will be that of world community. Lesser cultural units must in the end acknowledge their mortality. It cannot be avoided. As Jean-Paul Sartre observed, "Not to act is also to act," and the choice is not so much what lies ahead but how we accept it, struggling to the end or with a good will. As never before, young people, far more readily than their parents, are empathizing and identifying with the problems and aspirations of their generation worldwide. With luck, national loyalties will yield to world ones and a global society will result while this earth is still a fit place for habitation. This is a lesson that must be learned—the sooner the better.

The Prospects for World Government

Today, most of the world's population exists under a handful of stabilized, almost invulnerable centers of law, order, and, if occasion demands, violence. They include the USSR and her satellites, China, Western European democracies, the United States, and India. Most of these, together with the remaining less-well-organized areas of the globe, are involved in numerous international organizations. The United States belongs to over fifty, all planning at the global level with a considerable consensus as to basic social and human needs. Yet this unprecedented web of world law and order contains no coercive force to prevent violent adjustments between classes, religious groups, or nations. Herein lies the great obstacle: the insistence on national sovereignty. Powerful nations fear that the sacrifice of sovereignty will deprive them of present international advantages and that they will be less secure than when protected by their own military forces. They are suspicious that judgments made by a world authority will be disregarded by other nations or that those decisions will jeopardize their own national interests. These are very real concerns and will not be easily shed. Many a statesman will say, "If I only had to speak in my own account, I would take the chance," but then comes a sense of caution and security. The people must be safeguarded. Not that precedents are lacking when outstanding leaders have convinced their followers to join in common cause. The United States and other national federations are the result of such decisions to join together. Usually these groupings are responsive to a common threat, but until the dangers inherent in failing to join together are more vividly evident, the process will be resisted.

There must be no illusions about the straight path to world community. Much social experimentation will come first, a great many withdrawals into outmoded formulas, with the best hope being that none of these retrogressions will be fatal before humanity arrives at eventual agreement. Assuming that in its present anarchy, national states will never achieve stability, the movement toward unification may be encouraged by grave natural disasters, the gradual deterioration of the environment, war, or a combination of these. The world might be united from above by a single powerful state. Either the United States or the Soviet Union might remodel the world in the image of its particular society, but for one to so prevail over the other implies war or a terrible risk of war. A joint American-Russian domination is feasible. These two countries have their disagreements but they also have their areas of cooperation, their economic and cultural exchanges. Such a partnership could hardly make for stability in the long run, nor would it be acquiesced in by the rest of the world.

The only workable approach is some form of world congress supported by all nations. No doubt the idea is Utopian, but what is the choice? Albert Camus wrote: ". . . To reply once more and finally to the accusation of Utopia: for us, the choice is simple—Utopia or the war now being prepared by antiquated modes of thought. . . . Skeptical though we are (and as I am), realism forces us to this Utopian alternative. When our Utopia has become part of history, as with many others of like kind, men will find themselves unable to conceive reality without it. For History is simply man's desperate effort to give body to his most clairvoyant dreams."

What those in positions of power may scorn as Utopia is now the basis for human survival. Countless generations of our ancestors have strengthened their hold on this planet by refining their capacity to cooperate in ever-larger groups. To secure that grip finally, we must accept cooperation on a global scale. For certain functions, sovereignty must be scaled up to global institutions. For others, it might well be scaled down to fit the needs of more local communities. No such supranational authority now exists. The world was closer than it is now to realizing such an international organization in 1945 with the optimistic birth of the United Nations. Since that time the UN has retrogressed into relative impotence, but the structure remains and could, with the active cooperation of all its members, be transformed into the seat of world government.

The functions of a revitalized United Nations or comparable agency have been variously discussed. Most important are the following: (1) The supervision of general, proportionate, and complete disarmament at the national level with the substitution of a world peace force strong enough to suppress the use of force in international relations. (2) The legal and political means to settle peacefully international disputes, via an international court. This additionally presupposes a supranational body of world law upon which equitable decisions can be based. (3) A world development organization concerned with population control, the distribution of the world's limited resources, and the maintenance of ecology. The primary task of balancing the global ecological budget is to ensure that total consumption does not exceed nature's ability to renew. (4) A financial department to enforce agreed-upon allocations of operating expenses.

Given the necessary elements of world government, how are they to become a reality? The process at present, if it can be described as a process, is exceedingly gradual and this is probably how it will come to pass: in slow, small, separately negotiated stages. People must be brought slowly to consider the merits and realities of world government. They must become accustomed to the idea. World rather than national symbols are necessary, eventually a world currency, just as we are getting used to universal units of weights and measures. United States policy-makers should not reject out of hand as propaganda Soviet overtures regarding global negotiation. Undoubtedly these gestures have a propaganda feature, but to reject them automatically is a step backward and a tacit admission to the world's people that the United States has nothing convincing to offer. To isolate and finally eliminate war, every effort, however modest, should be made to build a sense of world community. There are many areas where this can be done, and to a degree is being done in terms of sporting events, artistic performances, technical and scientific missions, college study abroad, and service in the Peace Corps. Intensified international contacts of this sort, although they have their bad moments, help to diminish distorted and stereotyped thinking about foreigners. Where conflict does exist, contact helps to reveal it and in the long run breaks down preconceived ideas.

Despite the general, if reluctant, acceptance of world government by osmosis, there are valid arguments for the so-called big-jump approach. Its adherents say, "What have the gradualists accomplished in the last thirty-five years?" Where tangibles are concerned, the criticism is valid. In brief, their thesis is as follows: by developing a comprehensive package of proposals, a picture of world order can be shown to all states who would recognize that it is to their overall benefit to move quickly from the present limp-along system to one of government on a world level. It sounds good in print, but in practice such a big jump would undoubtedly require a conjunction of idealistic, near-messianic leaders such as the political systems of this world have seldom produced, and a crisis vital to world-wide survival—a thermonuclear war or a breakdown in the ecology, which of course is occurring only gradually at this time.

A Limited World Agency

Though desirable, the complete surrender of national sovereignty at this time is inconceivable. However balanced world government would be in terms of representation, a participating nation would at times be in the minority. How would citizens of the United States, or that geographical area that had formerly been the United States, react to a graduated worldwide income tax where they were contributing ten times the amount of the average Chinese? Such socioeconomic questions facing world government would be far more difficult to deal with than the purely military ones. With this in mind, it has been proposed that, instead of attempting an all-inclusive world government, a limited agency concerned solely with restricting war be established. From the standpoint of mere survival this is of most immediate importance, for without the continuance of life other values cannot be appreciated. Once the peoples of the world have accepted world community at this elemental level, then other fears—of Africans that their lands would be exploited by industrial nations; of industrial nations that their barriers against indiscriminate immigration would vanish; of Communists that their subjects would be seduced by capitalism's consumer goods—all could be dealt with in their own good time. History has shown ad infinitum that confused crowds will butcher each other unless men of greater vision intervene. No rational person can find any merit in global war, though few of these people have the courage to act on these convictions. Yet that should be an adamant starting point: no more violence as a solution to world problems. The time-honored rules of self-help and neutrality in times of upheaval must be abandoned. The elements necessary to replace war as a means of change among states are three: disarmament, a world police force, and a judicial body capable of resolving disputes.

Disarmament

Today the United States is armed to the teeth. It used not to be. Since 1818 our border with Canada has been demilitarized, and for a long time armaments were regarded as an outgrowth of the decadent European system of power politics. All that vanished with World War II, and in 1955 Winston Churchill summed up the situation in an address to the British House of Commons: "We may now have reached a stage where safety will be the sturdy child of terror and survival the twin brother of annihilation." His "balance of terror" has been tremulously maintained ever since. Humanity stands by values, real or imagined, for which it will fight to extinction—a curious position from whence disarmament is dismissed as an unrealistic fancy. Yet is it in fact any more Utopian than preserving peace with terror? History points out that arms races end in war. Unilateral disarmament and the few cautious shufflings toward mutual disarmament thus far attempted have never precluded war either, though their scroll of failure is far shorter than that of the warriors. To be for or against disarmament is not a practical stance. The military planner who myopically sees only the perpetual arms spiral is no more realistic than the dedicated pacifist who expects a warring world to remake itself by a sheer act of will. The choice is like trying to cure an alcoholic by giving him a case of vodka on the one hand and a dressing-down on the other.

Since World War II there has been considerable talk about disarmament, but no sovereign nation welcomes a reduction of its own strength unless its position relative to that of other nations is at least maintained. Just after World War II, while the United States still had a monopoly on atomic weapons, it seemed willing to break these rules subject to the so-called Baruch Plan. Composed in early 1946, the Baruch Plan suggested that the United States would turn over managerial control of the atomic industry to an international authority and, once that authority had the power to inspect for violations at the national level and if need be impose sanctions, would get rid of its stockpile of atomic bombs as well. Of course, at this time most of the nations involved in the plan were capitalistic supporters of the United States, which was confident of being a dominant influence on the international authority. At least, that is how it looked to Soviet Russia, which dismissed the proposals as a diplomatic trick to perpetuate U.S. military superiority. Its alternative suggestion was for the United States to dismantle its atomic bombs within three months and agree mutually that such weapons would never be used, without any provisions for inspection to determine that atomic bombs were not being made secretly. That the United States refused to surrender a position of strength for naked promises is not surprising. Negotiations dragged on. It must be admitted in behalf of the Soviet Union that even after it developed the atomic bomb and seemed to have taken the lead in terms of intercontinental ballistic missiles, it continued to urge a ban on all forms of these weapons.

The several flies in the ointment became apparent on March 1, 1964, when both countries unveiled their disarmament proposals. The Soviet suggestion urging simple world law calling for disarmament and forbidding aggression between states sounded delightful except that it relied on the good faith of the nations involved and provided virtually no international authority to make sure it worked. The U.S. proposals leaned the other way, raising so many questions regarding inspection of weapons systems as to seem to lack a sincere intent to achieve disarmament. Since then armament, not disarmament, has remained the chief concern in Moscow and Washington. "We arm to parley" as Churchill observed, and yet the importance of disarmament to the two superpowers remains undiminished. The burden of defense—no guarantee against mutual annihilation—grows annually. How much safer and more economical it would be if the burden could be transferred to a strong world body. Yet neither superpower is ready to make a concession, which would automatically be seen as a sign of weakness and a loss of strategic advantage.

In the United States it is axiomatic to blame the Russians for the failure to achieve disarmament, yet no nation in history has ever so fervently proclaimed a craving for disarmament. Is it all just Soviet propaganda? Writing at the end of World War II, the Russian historian Eugene Tarle observed: "From time immemorial the idea of disarmament has been one of the most popular means of dissimulating the true motives and plans of governments. The explanation of this is very clear. . . . Every proposal for the limitation of armaments can always count on wide popularity and support from world opinion." Is there no more to it than that?

The Czars of Imperial Russia always maintained the biggest armies in Europe, yet as early as 1816 Alexander I was suggesting a reduction of forces and, as the century was about to close, at the first Hague Conference Czar Nicholas II was calling for lasting peace by limiting existing armaments. Communism at its inception had little to say on the subject. Karl Marx occasionally said he favored it with reservations, primarily because the Czar was its main booster. Marx's collaborator Friedrich Engels began by branding disarmament as hopelessly Utopian, but, eventually sensing that the arms race led to disastrous war or economic bankruptcy, he became a firm adherent.

The development of Communist dogma then passed into Lenin's hands. Initially he gave lip service to a resolution by the Communist International calling for disarmament. Later he changed, writing in 1916 that disarmament was only feasible in a classless society and that that society could only come about after the bloody triumph of communism over capitalism. This remained dogma until after World War II, by which time capitalism had shown a surprising longevity and a retreat from the naked economic imperialism with which communism associated it. Then, too, the advent of the atomic bomb forced even the most rigid Communist to question whether capitalistic greed was sufficiently insatiable to push the capitalists into wars of suicidal annihilation. Not only in theory but in practice, there are good reasons to believe that peace and disarmament are in Soviet Russia's best interest today. Though Russian mothers are not likely to croon their babies to sleep with "God Bless America," a thirty-five-year period of coexistence since World War II suggests that there is room on the planet for both systems. During that time both systems have derived greater success from avowedly peaceful methods than through the use of force, though Russia's periodic acts of aggression, including the recent invasion of Afghanistan, leave some doubt as to Soviet intentions. With a smaller gross national product than the United States, defense spending represents a greater burden to the Soviet economy. For that matter, as industry there is state-controlled, there is no problem with unemployment if workers are removed from armament construction. Then, too, there is the gradual spread of thermonuclear capabilities to other nations, a progression that must limit both Moscow's and Washington's control of the world situation. So long as an agreement offers greater security than can be derived from the present standoff in the overkill arsenals that are now relied upon, it is reasonable to expect that the Russians will press for it with cautious sincerity. Such is the nature of SALT (Strategic Arms Limitations Treaty), which went on laboriously during the 1970s in the hope of making a start in curbing the pell-mell arms race.

The United States has the same incentives as the Soviets in limiting the arms race, even a distinct advantage in achieving peaceful economic competition where she has a commanding lead in producing consumer goods that have world appeal. One problem not shared by Russia is that of resettling the labor force employed by the armaments industry. Clearly the readjustment period would be a difficult one, but in terms of the larger picture, massive military investments are a costly form of insurance that forces the United States to lag behind the democracies of Western Europe in furnishing basic social services to the people. Surely the work force could be better employed in upgrading the environment, urban renewal, building medical facilities, and so forth, than in unceasingly grinding out weapons.

Yet man remains a weapon-loving creature. Weapons seem fixed in his very biology. The fact that the personal and selective bludgeon has evolved into an impersonal and indiscriminate thermonuclear bomb does not change his mentality. No leader, of whatever charisma, can press ahead with significant disarmament unless he has the people behind him. Whether the above hypothesis is true or false, it appears it is in accord with recent SALT-type efforts to gain agreements between nuclear powers rather than to attempt to ban the fearful weapons entirely. All that can be said of arms limitations talks is that dialogue between superpowers is better than suspicious silence, and modest agreement is preferable to none, even though such talks presuppose the continuance of the arms race.

Having come to a rather pessimistic conclusion about general disarmament, mention of unilateral disarmament by one superpower regardless of the conduct of its rivals may seem at first glance the height of absurdity. Only a few pacifists dare suggest that any of the world's stronger nations would have the courage to disarm in the presence of their enemies. What would happen? The answer depends on when the question is asked. In the 1950s, according to conventional wisdom, if the United States had let down its guard, the Soviet Union would have "taken over." What if Russia had disarmed then? Such a possibility seemed so remote in American circles as to warrant little speculation, though the chances are that the United States would not have "taken over" the Soviet Union. To what purpose?

Today, with tempers cooled a bit, what would be the result? The popular phrase today is "atomic blackmail." If invasion is no longer contemplated, would the unarmed nation be pushed around internationally and reduced to impotence? Or would it rather gain the respect and admiration of the world? This seems as likely a possibililty, but the risks cannot be discounted. Realistically, until vast numbers of people have experienced a change of heart sufficient to give their support to a leader of uncommon conviction and faith in humanity, unilateral disarmament is only a theoretical possibility.

Far short of such an achievement, there is the possibility of "unilateral initiatives." They have been proposed as an alternative to the SALT-type talks in which, as the Red Queen said to Alice in Looking Glass Land, "Here, you see, it takes all the running you can do, to keep in the same place." This is in reference to the policy of creating new terror weapons as "bargaining chips" for future disarmament talks, the arm-to-disarm approach. A policy of unilateral initiatives, on the other hand, would have one side very publicly abandon an element of threat: that is, reduce certain forces, abandon certain weapons, while encouraging the opponent to reciprocity in kind. This, too, has not been tried; according to our conventional military definition of life it would be Utopian and naïve, but it is an idea that need not threaten security and, if reciprocated, could initiate a sane redirection of the arms race.

An International Police Force

Disarmament, should it ever be achieved by less than saintly men, would require an international organization to maintain order in the world. This peace force—in an agency concerned only with preventing war—would have a right to intervene only when attacked, when a nation refused to allow inspection for illegal weapons or otherwise violated the disarmament plan, or when one nation brought force against another. Even so restricted, its task would be monumental, particularly in the initial phases when nationalistic sentiments were not yet reconciled.

Already, through United Nations intervention, peace-keeping forces volunteered by member nations have achieved stability in a number of international disputes. A step forward would be to create a minimal permanent force for immediate use. As few as one thousand well-trained and well-equipped soldiers could stabilize many international confrontations. Intervention by such a peace force within a nation-state refusing to comply with the rules of disarmament would be unprecedented, but it might be undertaken, much as the U.S. federal government involved itself during the civil-rights crisis in the South, by applying firm restraint and much television coverage, thus involving the pressure of world opinion.

A World Survival Court

With a peace force maintaining the world status quo, clearly an agency to supervise legitimate change and settle international disputes would be required, once war was no longer available to achieve that purpose. Even without disarmament or an international peace force there is a vital role to be fulfilled by a court of international law. To the extent that sovereign nations rationally agree that war must be prevented, they should also concur that the best way to settle disputes short of war is through the impartial application of a system of international law. The apparatus, the International Court of Justice, has long existed at The Hague, and it is well qualified to do the job. Nevertheless, it is seldom busy. Only a third of the United Nations members have acquiesced in the court's jurisdiction and, in most cases, only subject to extensive reservations. If the court were to be used more extensively, how, without a peace force, could it guarantee its decisions? The same question arose regarding the Supreme Court of the United States when it was deemed inappropriate for the Court to enforce its decisions against the individual states. Only the strength of public opinion was left to sanction its holdings. Never before had sovereign states acquiesced in the idea that law alone, not force, would resolve their disputes. Human sacrifice and slavery have been eliminated largely by the concentration of public opinion. War as the primary settler of disputes could be eliminated in the same way.

This does not imply that conflict or struggle could or should be eliminated. Neither world law nor the human condition ever will arrive at a point of fixed perfection. Both must evolve and change, but a system of world law would eliminate violence as the crude means of bringing it about. Of course, the vast web of problems that obstructs our future cannot be brushed aside by new international organizations alone. Even before a framework of such institutions can be constructed, changes of a very fundamental nature must take place in our system of priorities and values.

Directions to Be Encouraged

There is a story about a traveler lost in the Irish countryside who, upon asking a farmer the quickest route to Dublin, received this reply: "Faith, if it's Dublin you're after, this is no place to be startin'." The world today, beset as it is with perils and animosities, may be no place to find the way to peace, but it's hardly the time to give up. If we are not to have world government or even a world peace force, there are preliminary trends and/or directions to be encouraged.

General education is one, and in some areas a broadening of that term to enlarge what has become dangerous thinking in narrow stereotypes. Since war is often an expression of frustration and anger against changes in one's environment, the better informed a people are, the more adaptable they will be in abandoning outworn ideas and accommodating themselves to modifications in their life-style. A person is simply more sensible in accepting compromise when the reasons behind it are understood.

Certain words, if not necessarily to be redefined, certainly should be intelligently explored beyond that cluster of emotional slogans which noisily pretend to represent them. Take these three: Patriotism, the Enemy, Soviet Russia. Patriotism is accepted as one of the higher virtues; it is a state of mind associated with such expressions as "My country, right or wrong," "Fifty-four Forty or Fight," "Give me liberty or give me death," and "Damn the torpedoes, full speed ahead." Patriotism is equated with courage and codes of honor, with leaping to arms in response to the nation's summons. Yet patriotism and doctrines concerning one's country's good are subjects open to discussion, areas in which a great range of opinion operates. From earliest childhood one assumes that the only proper reaction to a threat to one's country is a resort to war. Courage and conscience are automatically on the side of war. In such a context, disarmament becomes a symbol for cowardice, weakness, and surrender. The links among courage, patriotism, and the resort to war are very strong. They should at least be explored, if not broken. Inherent, too, in the word *patriotism* is the assumption that the sovereignty of the group is permanent and from the point of view of the group members must remain so, as a matter of life and death. Such a belief where the present-day nation-state is concerned is unmitigated totalitarianism, the greatest threat possible to true democracy. In actuality, extending a degree of sovereignty to a larger world agency would not doom that nation any more than states, counties, cities, or towns vanish when they are part of a larger unit of loyalty.

In war, the good patriotic citizens of one nation fight "the Enemy," always an evil abstraction, sometimes singled out by an equally abstract and deprecating nickname. "The Hun is always either at your throat or at your feet" was Winston Churchill's way of describing Germans in general. "Hun" was the British term for the Enemy in World War I. The French preferred "Boche." The enemy in Vietnam were "gooks," and "gooks" were sufficiently abstract as not to be killed but "wasted." Abstraction makes war that much more endurable.

Such abstractions are, of course, functions of ignorance, and the educated soldier has difficulty grasping the unreasonableness of such stereotyped patterns of hatred. Once he has learned to reason concretely and is aware of historical causes and the guilt of both sides, he is very likely to sympathize with his potential foe. Here is a great hope, that education supplemented by modern conditions of travel, communication, and the sharing of knowledge will make it more difficult for citizens of one country to passionately accept devil images of "the Enemy."

After World War II, "the Enemy" and "Soviet Russia" were nearly interchangeable terms in the United States, except that the latter carried the connotation of a way of life which at any moment might be thrust upon Americans and which wasn't worth living. All this was summed up in the popular slogan "Better dead than Red," implying that extinction is preferable to life in a Communist system. But even if the average Russian is severely restricted in his political and public life, has fewer consumer goods, and so on, he eats, loves, marries, has a family, all the basic ingredients of a decent life. Still, it would be as unreasonable to expect the United States government, as the leading exponent of modern capitalism, to support a system of education that endorses communism as it would be to expect Soviet Russia to expound the merits of capitalism in the classroom. Yet if the human race is to have any tomorrow and the day after, the vehemence of such hostility must be modified to a level of criticism that permits cooperation on important international issues while recognizing the existence of irreconcilable differences. The point, as far as the individual is concerned, is not to exist by slogans which, in their partisan simplicity, are always a distortion of reality. Even in school today our ideas are shaped at best by regional values and perspectives. World history is seldom taught impartially in the United States and is undoubtedly subjected to even greater distortions in the Soviet Union. If freedom is indeed our most cherished right, we can retain it only if we possess the critical ability to evaluate existing standards without accepting those thrust upon us ready-made. That ability comes only with education, as distinguished from indoctrination. When a foreign country is being studied, its people's achievements should be as readily presented as their mistakes, their virtues ranked against their vices. To question "Better dead than Red" once amounted to an "un-American activity." If we have moved away from that polar extreme, what about the axiom "You can't put faith in any agreement made with Moscow"? There is a substantial truth in this, but the implication remains that the Soviet Union is uniquely perfidious, while in fact a careful study of international agreements will show that all nations keep those agreements which their leaders regard as beneficial, while they manage to break those which changed circumstances have rendered detrimental. This appears to be a fact of history, not a singularly Soviet perfidy, but it takes considerable education to arrive at that conclusion.

Channeling Aggression

Clearly a population that has been educated above the level where the most primitive slogans and stereotypes are blindly accepted is a population that cannot be stampeded into war without good reason. There is little argument on this score, but much more when aggression becomes the subject of discussion; and as always the parting of the ways hangs on the basic issue: Is aggression instinctive or learned?

The instinctivists go back to William James, and in terms of education would support his thesis in *The Moral Equivalent of War*. According to James, human beings are innately pugnacious, particularly young males, and an outlet is needed for this violent energy. James believed that the tame Utopias imagined by pacifists never provide sufficient outlet. On the positive side he sees merit in many of the martial virtues so long as their expression can be shifted from destruction to something constructive. "A permanently successful peace-economy cannot be a simple pleasure-economy," said James. "In the more or less socialistic future towards which mankind seems to be drifting we must still subject ourselves collectively to those severities which answer to our real position on the only partly hospitable globe. We must make new energies and hardihoods continue the manliness to which the military mind so faithfully clings." Ways should be found, according to James, for young males to express their courage and strength through a moral equivalent of war, and one that satisfies the lust for the heroic as war does. Once civilian life can furnish the attractions of idealism, equality, comradeship, adventure, and excitement as vividly as only war does, then it will no longer be easy to persuade people to fight a war. But just what is this moral equivalent to be? No single phenomenon would seem sufficiently vast to supplant the institution of war. The Peace Corps has been seen as one such outlet, the space race another. An organized attack on our faltering ecology might become another. Some theorists point to sport in ancient Greece and Rome as substitutes for war as a crowd phenomenon, and perhaps it is regaining the same role today on a global scale. If war is on the way out, then the survivors must be reckoned with, and if communities and nations must be rivals, then many experts regard international sporting events as doing nothing but good.

Channeling aggressive energies into constructive rather than destruction patterns is brought into question by those who view aggression as a learned phenomenon, particularly the idea that sporting events will siphon off violence. Sociologists note that combative sports are most common to combative and warlike societies, and that, rather than diminishing aggression, sporting events reinforce violence among participants and spectators alike. Such ideas seem to transcend the matter of whether or not it is an appropriate political gesture to boycott the Olympic Games and question, rather, whether or not they should ever be held at all.

Closely associated with this debate is that of letting children play with toy weapons and tin soldiers or watch violence on television or in the movies. Does it sublimate such conduct or does it reinforce it? Most psychologists seem to regard such forms of play as giving reassurance against anxiety, which says little about how that reassurance may later express itself. The overriding concern is with the anxiety itself. If parents rear .their children with humane love and consideration, the question of channeling an overabundance of aggression will not be a problem whether the child plays with toy tanks or stuffed teddy bears, watches war films or tearjerkers.

On the positive side, the behaviorists advocate the teaching of cooperation in preference to channeling aggressive behavior. They advocate games of cooperation rather than competition, though such games are often hard to find and most team activities, while emphasizing cooperation amid one group, focuses this cooperation as competition directed against another—the very essence of war itself. Perhaps more can be achieved at the individual level in teaching cooperation. At the moment it runs counter to the American ethic of excelling over others, of rising to the top against all odds. This does not mean that social cooperation cannot be taught and learned, eventually on a world scale. In fact, to a degree it is already being learned, not so much in the kindergarten or on the playing fields as among the worldwide businesses, which in the past have been associated with cutthroat economic competition.

World Business Trends

Traditionally, huge "defense contracts" are eagerly sought by industrialists for their high profit margins, by workers for the jobs involved. To this extent industry would seem, in Oswald Spengler's words, to be "the weapon of a beast of prey." Traditionally, too, it has been the task of government to protect its businesses against foreign competition to ensure full employment, a policy with potentially detrimental consequences as noted in the following lampoon by the Frenchman Frederic Bastiat: "To the Chamber of Deputies: We are subjected to the intolerable competition of a foreign rival, who enjoys such superior facilities for the production of light that he can inundate our national market at reduced price. This rival is no other than the sun. Our petition is to pass a law shutting up all windows, openings, and fissures through which the light of the sun is used to penetrate our dwellings, to the prejudice of the profitable produce we have been enabled to bestow on the country. [Signed] Candlestick Makers."

The idea is absurd, but is no more than an exaggeration of the fact that, to the extent a government protects its workers against foreign competition, it encourages inferior products at soaring costs.

Such time-honored protectionism has begun to go against the grain of today's big business, which increasingly overlaps national boundaries and seeks a world market. No longer is defense spending uniformly seen as a boon to business. It may at this point be keeping a few specialized industries afloat, but others recognize the production of weapons of mass destruction as economic "waste," which in turn fuels inflation. Not only is it waste, but it diverts government spending from what many believe should be its real priorities: the rehabilitation of large cities, the improvement of mass transit, better and cheaper medical services. The failure of the government, absorbed in the prospect of foreign wars, to invest in the American society itself is increasingly seen as detrimental to the investment climate.

An additional pressure toward international business cooperation comes from outside: our increasing dependence upon foreign sources for raw materials, coupled with the grudging recognition that the ages of exploration-colonization and exploitation are over. So the imperialistic marriage of business and the nation has fallen on hard times. While nationalism still stands for the competitive division of the human race into segregated groups, industrialism seeks to encompass the globe with ever-widening markets irrespective of political, racial, religious, or national barriers. The developing situation has been referred to as the imperialism of peace, quite the opposite conclusion to the old Communist view that capitalism leads to war, for it foresees the joint exploitation of the world by internationally united finance capital instead of the rivalries of national finance capital. In this situation, wars triggered for economic reasons are seen to belong to a prior age. For fully developed capitalism, they are at best troublesome and disruptive to free trade.

This transformation in the big-business outlook has largely come about since World War II. First there was the memory of the great prewar depression, which in large measure had been caused by economic protectionism between nations. After the war many states were obliged to give up colonial empires, notably Japan and Germany, which nevertheless, without the burden of massive military spending, have been the economic miracles of the postwar era. To this positive example was added the negative reinforcement of the debacle in Vietnam. Since that time the U.S. government has been under pressure to cut the costs of imperial wars, and a consensus referred to as business pacifism has developed, supporting alternative economic policies that would perform the functions presently performed by the Department of Defense. World War II bestowed economic benefits on Americans in general, but that is unlikely to be the case again, and corporate managers are accepting the fact that the quest for national interest via military methods is detrimental to profits and a threat to corporate property.

Simply put, nation-states are limited geographically, modern capitalism is not; and truly multinational corporations do better if they can free themselves from the prejudices associated with particular national identifications. They do better when they have considerable assets invested abroad to employ foreigners, when they count on foreign governments for protection, and when they actually detach themselves from nationalistic policies spawned in Washington. Such competition between big business and the state is just beginning. Where it will lead, only the future can show, but the international corporation enters the ring with certain assets. First is the fact that the nation-state has failed in its primary function, defending its population. Also, conducting imperial wars has become clearly uneconomical. No single nation can solve the major world problems, simply because they are international in scope, as are the multinational corporations. Perhaps with the best-educated minds being drawn into this world corporate structure, the good sense of the businessman will defeat the insanity of the warrior.

Yet the government is not without support in its struggle. There is that area of industry which increasingly depends on government subsidies to continue. Not only domestic industry but organized labor are backers of nationalism, for labor sees the multinational corporations taking advantage of lower wages abroad.

So the lines are drawn, with momentum at present on the side of the multinational corporations whose interests are served by peace and whose influence will be along lines of restraining military adventure. If the trend continues, ownership of most of the world's resources will presently be divided up among the multinational corporations of Western Europe and the United States and the state-controlled industries of China and the Soviet Union. Such a division might be described as the imperialism of peace, no doubt a condition preferable to imperialism in its older belligerent form. Yet it is scarcely an answer to the world's long-range problems that a clique of industrial powers should tacitly cooperate in exploitation and ever-expanding productivity, since the age of consumption and wastefulness must soon give place to an era of restraint incompatible with the nature of multinational industry.

The Peace Movement Today:
Christian Love, Reason, and Terror

Friedrich Nietzsche, the German philosopher whose adulation of the superman was so much responsible for Nazi thinking, nevertheless argued for a final breaking of the sword, if for no other reason than that men should prefer death twice over to being hated and feared. This is simply a negative restatement of Christian pacifism, which for nearly two thousand years has struggled ineffectively to reform the imperfect human animal. Only in a few relatively powerless sects has Christian love proved sufficient. As a global unifier it has failed. Within the Christian community it has been the source of as much violence as harmony, and to non-Westerners its symbols have proved alien, if not repugnant. Whereas Western Christianity professes "I am my brother's keeper," an ethic of action that justifies foreign intervention of the sort practiced in the past by the United States, a more Eastern outlook could be phrased, "I am my brother," which is far less subject to cynical distortion in this thermonuclear age. Even that does not go far enough, for the poisoning of other creatures and of plants by the testing of hydrogen bombs and the release of industrial wastes, regardless of whether we ourselves are poisoned in the process, should be put down as a crime against nature and a sin against whatever we construe God to be.

Where Christian love has failed, good sense has thus far fared little better. Spawned by the Age of Reason, world courts and congresses have been given pious lip service. It appears unlikely that war will ever be abolished by appeals to reason. Humanity has aspired to peace throughout its history, but this has not led to a decline in the occurrence or in the frightfulness of wars. The tame sensibilities of peace have never been able to match the group passions for destructive violence or the rationalization that war will bring advantages, that it can be won. Wars still can be won when they involve small formative states struggling with subnuclear weapons. They cannot be won by great nuclear powers fighting to the death. One American general characterizes such a third world war as a fire. A fire is something that can happen, but it cannot be won. It can only destroy.

One can hope, therefore, that to reason can be added the great dread and the knowledge that the issue is no longer victory or defeat but simply survival. The lesson seems very elemental, and yet we tend to accept a conventional and insane morality to the effect that "we will not resort to nuclear arms unless they do," which is another way of saying "We won't blow up the world unless they start it."

Amid this dangerous complacency, efforts should be made to push international compromise, justice in international quarrels, the alleviations of national antagonism through mediation and conference in the hope of prolonging year by year our shaky thermonuclear peace. Given enough time, wars may become as outmoded in the minds of men as they already are in practical fact. It is, in the last analysis, the minds of men that matter. If Waterloo for England was won on the playing fields of Eton, World War III, if it is not to be lost, may be averted in the classrooms of the United States and the Soviet Union.

The Study of Peace and War

Good schools pride themselves on offering courses in Latin, music, and Impressionist painting. At great universities research projects are financed by the government for the perfection of napalm and guided missiles. Why not research into the causes of war, and courses on that subject? Why departments of economics and biology, and never a department of paxology? Never has humanity shouldered a heavier responsibility than thermonuclear war. Albert Einstein recognized the danger when he stated that the atomic bomb changed everything except our patterns of thought. The solution is research and re-education. If this book has achieved nothing else, perhaps it has indicated the immensity of the peril under which we all live and our terrible ignorance of how this situation may be peacefully resolved. If we are to adapt and survive, we must know all that is possible about ourselves, particularly where the dynamics of war and peace are concerned.

A peace research movement was begun at the University of Michigan soon after World War II, with a periodical *The Journal of Conflict Resolution* predicated upon the belief that, while man is good, the system of war is evil and can, with knowledge, be changed. Considering its continuing relevance, the movement has had little success and "peace" courses at the college level have had very little funding, as they are seen to conflict with time-honored American foreign policy. The areas of ignorance are vast; the questions beg to be asked of experts drawn from all areas of science, politics, history, psychology, sociology, economics, and anthropology. At the individual level there are unresolved debates concerning the nature of aggression and the implications of cooperation versus competition. What are the appeals of war, to the individual and to the group? Why are there not detailed studies of men in combat by scientists free of military restraints, so that the results may be treated as medical information rather than as military secrets? The areas begging for exploration are nearly endless, and yet more time and effort at the college level is devoted to home economics.

Of course, the study is too big to be limited nationally. There should be a worldwide program, conceivably under the auspices of the United Nations, which could furnish transportation to experts in the related fields, as well as a network of appropriate research centers associated with universities and laboratories, with findings to be pooled and made available in all languages. To turn such an undertaking into a world society without violence is a distant and perhaps a forlorn hope, but that is no excuse for not trying. In the words of Camus, "Over the expanse of five continents throughout the coming years an endless struggle is going to be pursued between violence and friendly persuasion, a struggle in which, granted, the former has a thousand times the chances of success than that of the latter. But I have always held that, if he who bases his hopes on human nature is a fool, he who gives up in the face of circumstances is a coward. And henceforth, the only honorable course will be to stake everything on a formidable gamble: that words are more powerful than munitions."

The Future

The universe contains some one hundred billion billion fiery orbs, one of which is our sun. Whirling around these cosmic fires are an infinity of inert specks. Upon one of these swarms is the human race, building its pyramids and trade centers, its thermonuclear bombs and its dreams of a millennium to come. The fate of this speck in the larger scheme of things may be of no great consequence, but for the creatures dwelling upon it, there is nothing else. In the end the universe will have its way with the stars and planets, but within the foreseeable future the fate of the earth as an inhabitable planet is very much in human hands. Never before in its short history has humanity achieved such mastery over the elements, and never before has it been so helplessly at the mercy of its own creations.

There is no blissful millennium awaiting the human race as it approaches the twenty-first century. With good luck and a bit more sense than has been exhibited in the past, there *will* be a twenty-first century of recorded history. In that event it will show a record of hard times, of overcrowding, of dwindling resources, of an impoverished environment. Malnutrition grips nearly half of the world's population today. Tomorrow it will know starvation. The twenty-first century will see the fulfillment of the age of global confluence. Unavoidable tension between the countless sovereign states will undoubtedly aggravate those circumstances which traditionally cause wars. Change of a drastic sort is inevitable, and it is only a question of what form it takes—change by war or by new institutions that can make adjustments short of physical violence.

The history of the twenty-first century is not years in the future. It is being written now by rapidly expanding populations, by the impetuous spending of billions on weapons of annihilation, by the dumping of poisonous wastes into our delicately balanced and already imperiled ecology. It is not a happy record, and the question is: Do we make sacrifices for the future? A parent may do so for a child, but what of the yet unborn? There is very little emotional stake as the future extends away into the unknown, but if it is not to be a darkness beyond redemption the right time to start is rapidly passing.

The task is staggering, and it is very much up to this generation and the next to galvanize courage and wisdom unknown in the past. If skillful and moderate diplomacy can stave off World War III, new and unforeseen elements will eventually fill the international scene and new paths to peace may be open. Such is the hope of survival. It is up to every human being to turn that shaky prospect into a reality. Even with world peace assured, it will be achieved only at a great price in human liberty and alone will not resolve the great problems that question our ability to survive as a species.

The historian looking back on the next one hundred years, if there is such a historian, will record present-day capitalism and communism as a matter of record devoid of emotion and rallying cries. Today's differences, if we survive them, will be of little moment to people living then. If the historian does ex-

ist to tell of how this century ended and the next evolved, he
will tell of what amounts to a peace revolution embracing economics, nationalism, morality, and religion—a great awakening.

In 1776 the American colonies united in violent revolution
for the sake of liberty and independence, but when Jefferson
tallied up the inalienable rights of which no government could
legally deprive its citizens, life came first and liberty second. It
is life that we must fight for now, and if this peaceful revolution
is to succeed it must overcome many cherished "rights,"
among them the unfettered liberty associated with the American way of life. It must yield to a world way of life. Continuous
industrial growth, the very heart and soul of traditional capitalism, must be supplanted by doctrines of restraint and global
husbandry.

The peace movement of the 1960s failed in part because it
was born in hatred of the United States and extolled the victories of this nation's enemies. As with any powerful state, there
is much to hate in American society, none more than the mili-
tarist frame of mind that contributed to the Vietnam tragedy,
but hate is self-defeating. It cannot change the country for the
good. If the peace revolution is to succeed, it will do so as a
new style of enlightened patriotism that can reappraise the
citizen's role within the nation and the nation's place in the
world community. The peace revolution would move toward
real internationalism.

The success of a peace revolution in United States society is
no guarantee against war. Other nations are as capable of insti-
gating violence, but until American society is remodeled for
peace there is little hope of war being avoided. If the future
historian survives to write of this process, he will record a re-
assessment of the old aspiration to be and remain "number one
nation," an unattractive ambition in a world facing famine.

Before calling on one nation to accept true equality among
nations, and before man can be expected to respect and spare

his brother, he must learn to nurture those things in his environment which affect his life as much as his brothers do. This is no garden of Eden in which we can thoughtlessly graze, innocently confident of divine replenishment. It is a small finite planet, which we are rapidly befouling and divesting of its resources.

Is all this too much to expect? Human beings are not, and most never will be, saints, but we have shown enough goodness to wipe out slavery as a worldwide institution even though exploitation survives as a practice. Violence is very much a human quality. Men will go on beating their wives, hitting their children, and kicking their dogs. And it must not be forgotten that occasionally dogs bite back, children often outgrow their parents, and wives and mothers have ways of striking back. But since slavery has been put down, why not war as well?

If history is a matter of irrevocable destiny, then this book and the writings of future historians can but record the way that led to our doom. On the other hand, if human beings can change—and we must, like Camus, assume that we can—then, sorry as the present prospect for real peace may be, humanity can derive hope from the realization that only we ourselves stand in the way of relegating wars to past history. In the ever-changing world, human beings are the constant factor. Neither our social institutions nor our lethal weapons will determine the course of events. We ourselves are the final measure of all things, and in our minds and hearts will be fought the last battle.

A Guide for Further Reading

ARDREY, ROBERT. *The Hunting Hypothesis: A Personal Conclusion Concerning the Evolutionary Nature of Man.* New York: Atheneum, 1976.

————.*The Social Contract.* New York: Atheneum, 1970. Both controversial, entertainingly written studies on human aggression and violence.

ARON, RAYMOND. *The Century of Total War.* Garden City, N.Y.: Doubleday, 1954. A consideration of the new phenomenon of total war.

BARNET, RICHARD J. *The Roots of War: The Men and Institutions Behind U.S. Foreign Policy.* New York: Atheneum, 1972. Considers the President's circle of advisers and their responsibility for policy decisions, particularly those related to Vietnam.

————.*Who Wants Disarmament?* Boston: Beacon, 1960. Slightly dated but still relevant study of the back-and-forth posturing of the United States and the Soviet Union on the subject of arms limitation.

BIGELOW, ROBERT. *The Dawn Warriors: Man's Evolution Toward Peace.* Boston: Little, Brown (An Atlantic Monthly Press book), 1969. Very readable, persuasive study of war and peace.

BOHANNAN, PAUL, ed. *Law and Warfare: Studies in the Anthropology of Conflict.* Garden City, N.Y.: Natural History Press, 1967. A good anthropological survey, including a particularly interesting study of the warlike Jivaro Indians.

BRAMSON, LEON, and GOETHALS, GEORGE W., eds. *War: Studies from Psychology, Sociology, and Anthropology*. New York: Basic Books, 1964. A good cross-section of psychological and anthropological writings on war.

BROCK, PETER. *Twentieth-Century Pacifism*. New York: Van Nostrand, 1970. A detailed study of pacifism in this century, including the period of the Vietnam War.

BUMPERT, MARTIN. *Dunant, The Story of the Red Cross*. New York: Oxford University Press, 1938. A good, if dated, account of the most lasting organization to survive from the nineteenth-century peace movement.

CANETTI, ELIAS. *Crowds and Power*. New York: Viking, 1962. Original and thought-provoking on the subject of the human group and what makes it fight. A bit advanced for the beginner but a must for anyone who wants to pursue the subject.

CANTRIL, HADLEY. *The Psychology of Social Movements*. New York: Wiley, 1941. A study, from the social psychologist's point of view, of how a group is led into war, with emphasis on the Nazi movement.

CARR, ALBERT Z. *A Matter of Life and Death: How Wars Get Started or Are Prevented*. New York: Viking, 1966. A plea for compromise and statesmanship.

CHATFIELD, EARL CHARLES, ed. *Peace Movements in America*. New York: Schocken, 1973. Good, comprehensive study, especially of twentieth-century efforts, including more information on student groups than is found elsewhere.

CHEEVER, DANIEL S., and HAVILAND, H. FIELD JR. *Organizing for Peace: International Organization in World Affairs*. Cambridge, Mass. Houghton Mifflin, 1954. Considers the League of Nations, the United Nations, and other international organizations.

DUBOS, RENÉ. *Beast or Angel?* New York: Charles Scribner's Sons, 1974. A study of man's evolution from hunter-gatherer to agriculturist and the failure of the industrial age to achieve Utopia.

EDBERT, ROLF. *On the Shred of a Cloud.* University, Ala.: University of Alabama Press, 1966. Poetic, humane speculations on man trapped in the atomic age. Good section on man the hunter emerging into man the warrior.

FREUD, SIGMUND. *Civilization and Its Discontents.* Translated by James Strachey. New York: Norton, 1961. Freud's somewhat dated views on human aggression, important within their historical context.

FROMM, ERICH. *The Anatomy of Human Destructiveness.* New York: Holt, Rinehart & Winston, 1973. A difficult but very interesting psychological examination of violence among human beings.

GARDINER, ROBERT W. *The Cool Arm of Destruction: Modern Weapons and Moral Insensitivity.* Philadelphia, Pa.: Westminster, 1974. Modern man amid the arms race and the danger inherent in modern, long-range weapons that make war an impersonal and guiltless function.

GARDNER, RICHARD N. *In Pursuit of World Order.* New York: Praeger, 1964. Considers the UN, the World Court, and the developing world community.

GRAY, J. GLENN. *The Warriors: Reflections on Men in Battle.* New York: Harper, 1959. A very personal examination of the average soldier's response to war.

HEILBRONER, ROBERT L. *An Inquiry into the Human Prospect.* New York: Norton, 1974. A study of the population explosion and the world problems ahead.

HIGGINS, RONALD. *The Seventh Enemy: The Human Factor in the Global Crisis.* New York: McGraw-Hill, 1978. A dazzling projection of the hazards faced by the human race on this overcrowded, underfed, and overarmed planet. Suggestions for positive action.

HOLLINS, ELIZABETH JAY, ed. *Peace Is Possible: A Reader on World Order.* New York: Grossman, 1966. Good consideration of the arms race, the failures of the national state, and the various schemes for world order.

LAWSON, DON, ed. *Ten Fighters for Peace.* New York: Lothrop, Lee & Shepard, 1971. Essays on pacifists and others who have struggled against war.

LONG, EDWARD LEROY, JR. *War and Conscience in America.* Philadelphia, Pa.: Westminster, 1968. Considers ideas of the just war and degrees of war resistance, from "agonized participation" to "conscientious objection."

LOWELL, EDWARD J. *The Hessians in the Revolutionary War.* Williamstown, Mass. Corner House Publishers, 1970. An excellent study on the limited subject of mercenaries in the American Revolution.

MANTELL, DAVID MARK. *True Americanism, Green Berets, and War Resisters: A Study of Commitment.* New York: Columbia University Press, 1974. Fascinating psychological study of the two groups mentioned in the title and of the ways in which their natures and upbringing distinguish their attitudes toward participation in battle.

MAYER, PETER, ed. *The Pacifist Conscience.* New York: Holt, Rinehart & Winston, 1966. A sampler of the statements of individual pacifists over the ages, from ancient China to the present time.

MILLS, C. WRIGHT. *The Causes of World War Three.* New York: Simon & Schuster, 1958. An argument for responsibility in high places and a study of the dangerous patterns of thought that permit a drift toward war.

MONTAGU, ASHLEY, ed. *Man and Aggression*. New York: Oxford University Press, 1968.

————. *The Nature of Human Aggression*. New York: Oxford University Press, 1976.

MONTROSS, LYNN. *War Through the Ages*. New York: Harper, 1960.

O'BRIEN, CONOR CRUISE. *Herod: Reflections on Political Violence*. London: Hutchinson, 1978. Concerned mostly with terrorism and the right of a state to use violence against it.

SALT and American Security (booklet). Washington, D.C.: Superintendent of Documents, U.S. Government Printing Office, Nov. 1978.

SAMPSON, R. V. *The Discovery of Peace*. New York: Pantheon, 1973. A rather specialized history of pacifism, culminating in, and concentrating in depth on, the ideas of Leo Tolstoy.

SCHNEIDER, FRANZ, and GULLANS, CHARLES, trans. *Last Letters from Stalingrad*. New York: William Morrow, 1962. Letters sent home by doomed German soldiers at Stalingrad; a study of soldiers accepting or refusing to accept their fate.

SELG, HERBERT, ed. *The Making of Human Aggression*. New York: St. Martin's, 1971. More for the student of psychology than for the general reader, this is concerned with whether aggression is spontaneous or learned behavior.

SOMERVILLE, JOHN. *The Peace Revolution Ethos and Social Process*. Westport, Conn.: Greenwood Press, 1975. A rational protest against the war system that prevails in the world today.

STORR, ANTHONY. *Human Aggression*. New York: Atheneum, 1968.

VON LAUE, THEODORE H. *The Global City: Freedom, Power, and Necessity in the Age of World Revolution.* Philadelphia, Pa.: Lippincott, 1969. A thoughtful and original study that proposes a global outlook as the only alternative to race suicide.

WEINBERG, ARTHUR and LILA, eds. *Instead of Violence.* New York: Grossman, 1963. A good historical cross section of statements by pacifists and ideas for world government through the ages.

Index

213

Simons, Menno, 62
sit-in, 106
slavery, 4, 7, 15, 18, 35, 36, 206
Smucker, Donovan E., 78
Social Contract (Rousseau), 32
Social Gospel, 89
socialism, 81, 82
Soldier's Chaplet (Tertullianus), 57, 58
Solferino, battle of, 68
Somme, battle of the, 40
song duels, 13
South Africa, 66, 78, 90
Spaak, Paul-Henri, x
Spain, 8, 30, 34, 42–44, 77, 93
Spanish-American War, 8, 77, 78
Spanish Civil War, 42–44, 93
Spencer, Herbert, 78
Spengler, Oswald, 197
Spock, Dr. Benjamin, 108
S. S., 44
Stalin, Josef, 99, 100, 141
Stalingrad, battle of, 129
state, loyalty to (*see*, nationalism)
Steele, Harold and Sheila, 103
Stimpson, Henry L., 148
Stöhr, Dr. Herman, 94
Strategicon (Maurice), 23
Suez War, 165
Sultner, Bertha von, 69
Sumer, 7
Sunday, Billy, 27
Supreme Being, belief in, 110
Supreme Court, U.S., 32, 110, 190
survivors, 127
Sweden, 27, 30, 109
Syria, 19

Tarle, Eugene, 186
Taylor, Gen. Maxwell D., 151, 154, 169, 170
Telegraphic Union, 67
territorial imperative, 117, 118
terrorism, 170, 171

Tertullianus, Quintus Septimius, 57, 58
Test Ban Treaty, 105
"Thanatos" drive, 92
Thebes, Egypt, 7
Thebes, Greece, 19
thermonuclear war (*see*, nuclear war)
Thermopylae, battle of, 17
Third World, 30, 31, 147, 158, 162, 163, 165–168, 175–177
Thirty Years War, 60
Thoreau, Henry, 73, 74, 90, 106, 108
threats, 140, 141
Thucydides, 17
Tiamat, 14
Tokyo, 45
Tolstoy, Leo, 58, 71, 72, 82, 89, 130
Tolstoyan Vegetarian Society, 89
Torquatus, Titus Manlius, 21
total war, 33, 39, 41–44, 46
Total War (Der Totale Krieg) (Ludendorff), 39
Toward Perpetual Peace (Zum ewigen Frieden) (Kant), 61
tribal life, 3–6, 10–13, 130, 131
Troy, 16, 17
Truce of God, 24
Truman, Harry S., 45, 47, 48, 97, 101, 139, 143
Tupamaros, 170
Turks, Turkey, 24–26, 104
Twain, Mark, 78

Umma, 14
Unamuno, Miguel de, 43
uniforms (*see*, military uniforms)
Union for Transport and Railways, 67
United Nations, 48, 67, 98–101, 162, 181, 202
United States: American Revolution, 31, 32; civil rights, 103; Civil War, 1, 35, 76, 123; Congress, 38, 68, 69, 74, 82, 83, 86, 94, 101, 107, 112, 159; conscientious objection, 95, 96;